PIGEONS

GILLIAN HICK was born in Dublin and qualified as a vet there. She has practised for the past eleven years in both Dublin and Wicklow. She now lives with her husband and three children in County Wicklow where she runs her own veterinary practice. *Vet among the Pigeons* is her second book. Her first is *Vet on the Loose*.

THE BLUE CROSS

The Irish Blue Cross is one of Ireland's busiest and longest established animal welfare charities. The charity first began to provide its popular mobile clinic dispensary service in the mid-1950s. The small-animal services are provided for pet owners unable to afford private veterinary fees. The intervening years have seen the service grow and expand to the present-day ten weekly Dublin destinations. In 2009, 18,211 check-ups, treatments, vaccinations and procedures were delivered to the most needy pets attending its Dublin-based mobile clinics and newly established small-animal clinic at Inchicore. In addition, Blue Cross-trained horse ambulance staff provided a total of 399 service days at race meetings and equine events throughout Ireland, north and south. Funding for services and equipment is provided through the generosity of the general public, central and local government and the horse-racing sector.

VET AMONG The PIGEONS

Gillian Hick

THE O'BRIEN PRESS
DUBLIN

First published 2010 by The O'Brien Press Ltd,
12 Terenure Road East, Rathgar, Dublin 6, Ireland.
Tel: +353 1 4923333; Fax: +353 1 4922777
E-mail: books@obrien.ie
Website: www.obrien.ie

ISBN: 978-1-84717-208-2

British Library Cataloguing-in-Publication Data
A catalogue reference for this book is available from the British Library.

While this book is drawn from actual experience over several years of practice,
situations, locations and names have been changed.
Any resemblance to any person is entirely accidental.

1 2 3 4 5 6 7 8 9 10
10 11 12 13 14 15

Editing, typesetting, layout and design: The O'Brien Press Ltd
Illustrations: cover – Martyn Turner; page 1 – Aidan Cooney
Printed in the UK by CPI Cox and Wyman
The paper used in this book is produced using pulp from managed forests.

Acknowledgements

Firstly, my thanks to the many readers of *Vet on the Loose* who passed on their praise and good wishes. Sorry it's taken so long to write this one.

My thanks to the Irish Blue Cross who have allowed me to use the Ballyfermot clinic as a setting for some of the stories. The Blue Cross clinics are supported by voluntary staff and I was lucky to have had the privilege to work with two of the best in Gordon Nowlan and Eamon Cosgrave who, between them, have given almost eighty years' service to the pets of Dublin and their owners. Their good humour and compassion never once failed in all the nights, despite serving one of the busiest clinics in the inner city in all weather conditions and into all hours of the night.

My apologies, in advance, to the many nice equine vets and the ones who run decent equine courses! I was unlucky in my first experience described here, but thankfully have had good experiences since. Hopefully, the few remaining dinosaurs will soon become extinct!

While on the subject of vets, thanks to Ralf Seidewitz, my neighbouring colleague and friend, for picking up the pieces for me when my efforts to combine a twenty-four/seven on-call practice with rearing three young children didn't work!

My thanks to the staff of the O'Brien Press and in particular to Michael O'Brien, who allowed me to stay as a hobby writer, and to Ide, the editor, as she waded through pages of clinical detail and surgical procedures, not to mention my appalling spellings!

Thanks to Hillary and all the staff in our fabulous local book shop, Bridge Street Books in Wicklow town, for their ongoing support of *Vet on the Loose*.

Thanks to Mark Quinlan for his input in the accountant's meeting chapter. Mark, of course, in no way resembles the entirely fictitious boring suit in the story!

As always, my thanks to my husband, Donal, and three children, Molly, Fiona and Jack (who wasn't born for the timeframe of this book – sorry, Jack!). Thanks for the unending support and many cups of tea that were needed for the production of this book!

And, speaking of cups of tea, thanks to John Armstrong, who dropped in for a cup of tea one evening and ended up building a veterinary clinic – read all about that in the next book!

CONTENTS

PROLOGUE   PAGE 9

CHAPTER 1: LEAPFROG   13

CHAPTER 2: JED AND HIS FLUFFY PYTHON   25

CHAPTER 3: THREE LITTLE GIRLS AND THEIR DOG 35

CHAPTER 4: A HELPING HAND   51

CHAPTER 5: OUT OF THE HORSE'S MOUTH   62

CHAPTER 6: THE BALD EAGLE   75

CHAPTER 7: THE PYJAMA PARTY   84

CHAPTER 8: SPECIAL INDULGENCES   92

CHAPTER 9: TWIN LAMBS   98

CHAPTER 10: BEAUTY – OR THE BEAST?   107

CHAPTER 11: A DIFFERENT CONSULTATION   131

CHAPTER 12: THE FILLY FOAL   141

CHAPTER 13: A CASE OF BUMBLE FOOT   160

CHAPTER 14: A NASTY FRACTURE   170

CHAPTER 15: THE WHITE STUFF   191

CHAPTER 16: A TEMPERAMENTAL VEHICLE   201

CHAPTER 17: THE BEWITCHING HOUR   216

CHAPTER 18: NEW ARRIVALS   230

CHAPTER 19: NOT BAD FOR A FIVER!   241

PROLOGUE

The phone rang. Slug, my faithful canine assistant since I first qualified as a veterinary surgeon, looked up, expectantly.

'No, Slug. We're off duty,' I reminded her, following her gaze to the cherubic four-week-old baby, concentrating intently on studying her fingers in the cradle nearby. Motherhood had put a temporary hold on our veterinary career. Still, every time the phone rang, Slug jumped to attention.

'So, Gillian! How are all the sleepless nights going?' boomed John, a vet from Dublin for whom I had worked a few weekends over the previous years, usually at last-minute notice.

'Well, it's easier to get up at night to feed a baby than calve a cow,' I replied, leaving out the bit about how, after calving the cow you could go straight back to sleep instead of endlessly lying awake, wondering if that tiny creature beside you was still breathing, and equally afraid to breathe yourself in case you woke her.

'Ah, but you're probably getting fed up sitting at home at this stage. Do you good to get out of the house for a bit.'

I had a feeling I knew where this was headed. 'Well, no,

actually,' I insisted, firmly. 'Molly is only four weeks old. Maybe in another month or two.'

The voice on the other end of the phone was dismal. 'So, no chance you'd do a clinic for me this Wednesday, then?'

'No. Absolutely none. Not a hope.'

And that was how I found myself, at four o'clock the following Wednesday afternoon, hunting desperately among the Babygros for my stethoscope and rooting out my white coat from the maternity wear.

But only for an hour ... maybe even half an hour, I reassured myself, feeling slightly tearful at the thought of baby Molly, comfortably swaddled in the apprehensive arms of her father, blissfully unaware of the abandonment that was about to take place.

With debating skills that would have served him well in the Senate, John had convinced me to cover his weekly stint at the animal welfare clinic. Although I had heard of the Irish Blue Cross, to my shame I was ignorant of their purpose and work. John had explained to me that they ran a series of subsidised clinics throughout the inner city to bring veterinary care to the pets of those who couldn't afford it. My job for tonight was to go out with the mobile veterinary clinic and tend to the 'handful or so' of cases that would arrive at the Ballyfermot clinic.

'A couple of quick vaccinations and the odd itchy dog,' he reassured me. 'You'll be in and out in no time.'

By the time I had travelled out to Ballyfermot and met up with the mobile clinic, I had been away from home for an hour already and was desperately trying to stop myself from ringing just to check that all was okay. I was ready to bolt. Just a couple of itchy dogs, I reminded myself. Another few minutes and I'll be on my way home again.

Being unfamiliar with the area, I was surprised, as the Blue Cross ambulance pulled around the Kylemore round-about, to see a vast crowd of people lined up along the pavement. I scanned the area trying to see where the local football match might be held, but the surrounding concrete jungle offered no clues.

'Good crowd tonight,' commented Gordon, the volunteer driver for the clinic, as he pulled in alongside them.

'What match is on?' I asked, aware that in my angst-ridden silence I was probably appearing unfriendly.

'What match?' he asked. 'There's no match on tonight.'

Then it became obvious to me that not only was the footpath filled with enough people to support a good-sized football team but that these people were accompanied by an array of squalling puppies, yowling cats and oversized mongrels with the odd suspicious-looking cardboard box thrown in for good measure.

I looked at Gordon in horror.

'This,' he indicated, waving his arm expansively across the sea of expectant faces, 'is your audience.'

The 'in and out in no time' ran to a full hour and well into the second as I vaccinated and bandaged and prescribed tablets and doled out advice to what seemed like hundreds of pet owners. I didn't even have time to dwell on the image of John's smug face as he lay in his Spanish villa, enjoying the peace and tranquillity. Luckily, neither did I have time to dwell on the face of a hopefully sleeping baby.

It wasn't until one client left me with the all-but-forgotten refrain of 'Thanks very much, doc!' that I felt a grin slowly spreading across my face. Despite the long months out of work, the path worn to the National Maternity Hospital in Holles Street where I had become yet another unidentifiable mum, the frequent check-ups and weighings and measurings – the vet had returned!

For the rest of the clinic I came alive, sleepless nights forgotten, all fears of returning to work a thing of the past. With the last bandy-legged pit-bull lurching down the steps of the clinic, it seemed as though I had never been away.

As I drove back the miles towards home, though, the feeling of satisfaction was gradually overtaken by panic over what would await me. I could already envisage the scrunched-up little face, blotched and reddened from hours of incessant screaming. For the last few miles I could almost hear the indignant roaring in my ears and was breaking out in a sweat by the time I screeched to a halt in the driveway. As I opened the front door, the silence was deafening. This was worse than I had anticipated. Frantically, I burst into the sitting room and my eyes came to rest on the cradle, pulled over beside the large armchair, where husband, daughter and dog all lay snoozing happily, oblivious to my worst fears.

CHAPTER ONE

LEAPFROG

I finally resumed my regular job as the third vet in Riverside Veterinary Clinic, a mixed practice based in County Wicklow. My boss, Seamus, was an experienced vet, and my colleague, Arthur, had four year's more experience than I had. It seemed a lifetime since my short break for maternity leave and life went on as usual at a hectic pace at the clinic. I had been back in the thick of things for a good few months now. I could hardly believe that Molly was almost eighteen months old already!

One day, at a nearby four-hundred-and-fifty unit dairy farm, my visit coincided with the arrival of a tour bus of seventy or so kids from a south Dublin primary school on a mission to find out where their daily milk came from. The fact that my job for the day was to collect a semen sample from a bull to check his fertility before the season began was unfortunate. Although my patient was keen, and a dainty little Friesian cow stood by, ready and waiting to assist, I didn't rush in. The kids, all decked out in a multicoloured display of virgin wellies, were enthralled by the scene that lay before them. The little cow, obviously less concerned than me by their arrival, pulled greedily at an errant wisp of silage and raised her tail to dump a steaming deposit, quickly dispelling any romantic notions the children might have had about farming life.

The teacher, all decked out in immaculate tweeds and pristine boots, assuming I was from the farm, called for my attention.

'Oh, it's so good of you to have us out today,' she blustered. 'You've no idea how much the children have been looking forward to it. I'm a country woman myself, you see, and I thought it would be wonderful for them to get to see a real farm. Of course, it's not the same now,' she lamented, largely to herself as no-one seemed to be listening to her. 'When I was a girl, every cow had a name and we knew them all; not like now, with great ugly numbers on their backs and plastic tags in their ears.'

I thought back to the last time I had been in this yard, scanning a batch of heifers. I had overheard a heated argument between Richard and his elderly father as to whether number 435 (or Scruffy, as she was known), was an offspring of number 320 (Annabel, daughter of Lucy) or number 279 (Thatch, to Richard and his father), both of whom were sired by Butler, who could be traced back to Richard's grandfather's day. Despite the Department of Agriculture's best efforts at recording and traceability, nothing could match the mental records of a farmer who took pride in his stock.

'Would you mind telling us what you're doing today and,

maybe, what is a normal day for you in your life as a farmer?' continued Miss Clark, the teacher, interrupting my musings.

'Oh, well, I'm not a farmer at all, I'm afraid,' I told her, anxious to get on with my job as soon they were all safely out of sight.

'Oh, but of course you are a farmer,' she assured me, patting me gently on me arm. 'To me the farmer's wife is every bit as much a farmer as her husband.'

Much and all as I liked Richard, I went on to put the woman in the picture.

'You're right,' I replied. 'But, actually, I'm the local vet. I'm just here to carry out a few quick jobs.'

'The vet!' she exclaimed, clearly in absolute raptures. 'Boys! Girls! Come quickly!' she called out to her charges. 'I have some very exciting news for you. We really are the lucky ones today. This lady here,' she told them in a hushed voice, 'is the vet. A real live lady vet!'

The kids didn't look quite as excited as their teacher, who seemed to view me as one might view the arrival of a previously undiscovered exotic animal at the zoo.

Before I could pass a few pleasantries and get safely away, Miss Clarke continued, 'Maybe, girls and boys, if you're all on your best behaviour, this lady vet might like to spare us a few minutes to tell us about her job today.'

I looked briefly from the one-tonne mass of hairy bull to the dainty Friesian, to the bulky artificial vagina in my hand and back at the tender young innocent faces of the schoolchildren.

'Ah no, I'm afraid not,' I stumbled, desperately trying to

come up with some excuse as to why I wasn't going to give them a live performance. 'It's just that I have to collect a sample from the bull and I don't really think the kids should be in on it,' I confided to her. 'If I had been doing any other job it would have been fine, and of course they could have watched.'

'Oh, but the children would be delighted to see you take a blood sample, now wouldn't you, children?' she said, clapping her hands to regain the attention of the kids who seemed much more interested in the pea-hen and her litter of chicks than the local stud.

'Well, no, it's not a blood sample at all,' I whispered to her in increasingly urgent tones.

'Oh, a milk sample then – even better. Now everyone will be able to tell their parents tonight exactly where the milk comes from.'

I looked from her to the great big bulk of bull in the pen beside me and wondered fleetingly how much time she had spent on a farm in her childhood.

'Eh, no … not a milk sample. It's actually a *semen* sample I need, you see,' I eventually told her, hoping the case would rest and she would herd them off to look at some cute calves or something.

'Oh, I see … oh,' she continued, not quite as enthusiastically as before. 'How messy,' she concluded, but still, she was not to be deterred.

'Well, I suppose you could tell them all about that then,' she continued, obviously determined to make the most of the moment.

'Ah no,' I replied firmly. 'No. The bull might get

distracted. There's much better things for them to see on the farm. There's a shed full of tractors and harvesters and a load of newborn calves. I'm sure Richard will be out to you in minute to show you around.'

With perfect timing, he appeared out of the vast feed shed and greeted Miss Clarke warmly as though this little gathering was an annual event.

Miss Clarke was by now back in full glee and told the smirking Richard how wonderful an opportunity it was for the children to meet a 'real live lady vet'.

'And now, we're going to watch the vet take a sample,' she continued confidently. 'I think it's wonderful for the children to see these things first hand, don't you?'

I didn't. I really, really didn't; especially when I was the one doing the demonstration.

'No, I was just saying to Miss Clarke that they really couldn't watch,' I said, turning to Richard for support. 'Much too dangerous. I don't think your insurance would cover it or anything.'

'Not at all,' boomed Richard, clapping me genially on the back and waving a great big hand towards the cattle unit. 'Once the children stand in there well out of the way they can get a great view of everything.'

'How wonderful! Shall we get on with it, so,' concluded Miss Clarke before I could protest any further.

With a sense of something happening, the kids began to gather around. Greg, the stockman, who looked just as unenthusiastic as I did about the whole affair, led in the little cow while I stood brandishing the artificial vagina, or AV, as we called it.

Harry, the bull, was well accustomed to the procedure and approached enthusiastically.

'Now, children,' declared Miss Clarke, 'the lady vet is going to explain everything to you.'

Keeping my head down and ignoring her, I angled myself to accommodate the great big bull as he mounted the cow with an enormous grunt.

'Oh look,' squealed one of the little girls enthusiastically. 'The cows are playing leapfrog. I like playing leapfrog too.'

With another few grunts, Harry produced his sample and dropped back down to the ground with a triumphant bellow.

'He's grunting a lot,' added another girl. 'Did he hurt himself?'

At that stage, I decided the show was over and throwing back a hurried 'Can't let this get cold – have to dash,' I hopped out just in time as Miss Clarke began a lecture something along the lines of man-cows and lady-cows and baby-cows.

Richard had caught up with me by the time I got back to the car. The look on my face sent him off into great big deep-chested bellows of laughter.

'You are so dead,' I told him. 'Well you may laugh now but next time you want a real live vet to play leapfrog, do your own dirty work, don't bother coming for me!'

'Ah sure, the kids loved it,' he roared. 'Just think of them going off to write their school stories about the cows playing leapfrog and that's how you get the milk,' and he broke off again into peals of laughter.

*   *   *

As it was spring, I was in and out of Richard's yard on an almost daily basis from then on, but every time I arrived I threw a quick look around to check there were no coaches in the driveway. Richard always took great glee in relating the tale to anyone who cared to listen.

'I have a severe case of leapfrog up here,' he would roar down the phone whenever he rang the surgery.

With the bulk of the cows and heifers calved, it was well into summer when the time came for the annual TB herd test. Although a herd of that size with such a high proportion of cows to be blood-tested would usually send a sense of dread through me, the prospect of spending a day in Richard's yard was not so daunting. Both Richard and Greg were efficient stockmen and were no more interested in wasting time with dodgy crushes than I was. The metal crush which ran alongside the length of the hay shed could hold almost twenty cows and led out into an open expanse of fresh pasture, which greatly speeded up the whole process of loading and unloading. On the day of the test, I was happier still to see the bright sunny morning, not hot enough to hinder the progress, but just enough to make the task more pleasant. At least six other local farmers had been roped in for the job of loading and unloading the cows, and before long, the yard was filled with good-natured slagging in between the roars and bawls of the cattle.

Once the heifers and young stock had all been tested,

Harry, the bull, went next. His enormous frame was too great to fit into the crush, but Richard had welded a strong restraining gate in his bull pen. Having coated out for the summer, Harry looked magnificent. His thick coat was sleek and glossy and his powerful muscles rippled under the enormous hide.

'By God, he got over that dose of leapfrog well, anyway,' threw in Richard, much to the merriment of the other farmers, who had all heard the story.

Harry gave a few deep bellows as I subjected him to the indignity of clipping and measuring his skin before injecting the avian and bovine tuberculin. It took all of my strength to haul up the enormous tail to take a blood sample.

After a quick cup of tea and a sandwich in the hand, we carried on with the older cows and worked solidly – clipping, measuring, recording, injecting and blood sampling cow after cow after cow, until I felt they would never end. The mirth and merriment that had started the day gradually subsided as each batch of cows came through. I wasn't the only one who had started to fade, and by the last pen-full, it seemed as though we were all working in slow motion.

By the time we were finished, I hadn't the energy to get back into the car and go home for dinner. Generally, I didn't like to accept hospitalities on the day of a test. To me, it just seemed a little insensitive to sit and share a meal with a family when, in three days' time, you might be sending some of their stock to the factory if they failed the test. It was a different story on the day of the reading. If the test was clear, I always enjoyed at least a cup of tea in the relieved atmosphere that followed. If the test was positive, I would accept, if I was offered, as much to commiserate with the family. Despite only being a pawn of the Department of Agriculture, the vet was usually deemed responsible if some of the cattle were positive.

In Richard's case, though, I wasn't too worried as his farm was a closed one. They bought in no stock and grazed no common grounds with other farms. As far as I knew, they had never had a single reactor.

It took not only the decent dinner but a few mugs of tea before I felt sufficiently revived to gather myself and return home. The test had taken the best part of the day and I was happy to sink into a hot bath.

Three days later, I returned to the yard to read the test. In order to do this, all the cattle had to be loaded into the crush again and each animal had to be individually checked for any lumps or swelling around the site of the injection.

The same gang had gathered and we got through all the young stock in record time. As the cows were to be turned out to a different field, Richard opted for them to go next. Despite the efficiency of the operation, it was some time before the last cow ran through. Next we moved on to Harry, who by now was roaring indignantly at the disturbance of what should have been a quiet morning.

As I walked into the pen where he had already been enclosed by the gate, I stared in horror at the left-hand side of his neck. The top lump, which was the control injection of avian tuberculin, was barely palpable. The bottom lump, where I had injected the bovine tuberculin, had swollen to the size of a small golf ball. I stood with callipers in hand, knowing it was useless to measure the mass. Without a doubt, Harry was a reactor, and was destined for the slaughter-house.

I was suddenly aware of the frozen silence behind me, and in a flash it came to me that the mood hadn't been quite so jovial this morning. As though in a daze, I walked towards Harry and ran my hand over the oedematous lump, wondering why, oh why it had to be this one – this perfectly managed farm, this prize bull, bred from a generation of quality stock, this gentle farmer who until now I had never witnessed in anything but the best of form.

Cursing my cowardice, I stood mesmerised by the bull, unable to come up with the words to tell Richard that Harry, sired by The Dean (number 241) out of Tinkerbell (number 204), traceable back over at least five generations of stock bred by his father and grandfather before him, was on the way to the factory – to the factory where he would be slaughtered, have his lymph nodes slashed and analysed by an anonymous inspector, and then the tremendous carcass would be sprayed with an indelible dye, rendering it unfit for human consumption.

Richard said it before I did. 'That's him gone, so.'

I nodded numbly, aware of the strain in Richard's strong face not quite disguised by a scant smile.

'I can't believe it, Richard. I'm so sorry,' I mumbled inadequately.

'Not your fault,' he replied, matter of fact. 'No point in shooting the messenger, I suppose,' he continued weakly. His next words put a cap on what had turned into a nightmare. 'I don't think he'll be short of company. I think there's a few among the heifers that might be joining him.'

He was right. As Greg and the now-subdued batch of farmers ran the heifers through the crush, I tagged one after another of what should have been Richard's fresh stock with the ominous reactor tag. Not only was I sending *them* to the factory, but also the calves they carried, mostly due that autumn, the progeny of the luckless Harry.

In all, I tagged twenty-two cattle and watched as two of the local farmers herded them into a separate outhouse where they would await collection for the factory. As I put away my testing gear and washed my boots, I noticed Richard was missing from among the group. Feeling I couldn't just walk away without passing some comment, I looked around the sheds as the other men straggled away.

Making my way into the modern parlour, I could hear Richard before I saw him – greats racks of sobs seemed to tear him apart as he stood, head in hands, leaning up against the bulk tank.

I stood in horror, not knowing whether to leave him to his misery or approach him with futile words of comfort. He saw me before I could make up my mind. Quickly, he tried to pull himself together, and with a few deep gulps, the sobs reduced to an occasional quiver. He turned to me, wiping his face with a piece of the blue paper roll found in every dairy unit. As I came towards him, he offered his hand and I held it. We stood in silence for a few moments, hands clasped.

'Only those that have them can lose them,' he said with a watery smile – the oft quoted words that made me feel such a failure every time I heard them. 'Don't you worry about it,' he offered as we broke apart. 'Sure, we may as well have the cup of tea.'

Although I would rather have been anywhere else, there was no way I could refuse. It was a quiet threesome as Richard, Greg and I tried to swallow the hot tea.

With Richard's acute knowledge of his stock and their breeding lines, he knew without checking any tags or paperwork that in one short morning I had effectively wiped out his best breeding line.

By the end of the week, the Department officials were all over the place, offering vague theories as to why this particular outbreak had taken place. Many months later, a laboured report arrived outlining the theory that an infected badger might have contaminated the meal fed to Harry and his harem.

From that day, Richard, an ardent nature lover, has always had an aversion to badgers, taking any necessary steps to eliminate them from his farm.

For me, from that day on, I've always had an aversion to making grown men cry.

CHAPTER TWO

JED AND HIS FLUFFY PYTHON

The Irish Blue Cross clinic had served as my initiation back to work and I had come to enjoy my weekly jaunt across Dublin city so I decided to continue doing the Blue Cross work for the time being. John was only too delighted to take an extended break!

I always tried to arrive early for the clinic, which took place at seven o'clock every Wednesday evening. There was nothing worse than arriving to more clients than you would usually expect to see in a normal practice in a whole week. It was often difficult to judge the time of the journey there – tonight, when I didn't get stuck behind any tractors or slurry spreaders in Wicklow, or get caught up in a snarl of Dublin city traffic, I arrived in Ballyfermot at almost twenty to seven. At least that meant I could save a few people queuing if they had only come for advice.

I pulled into my usual parking slot and was relieved to

see that there was only one person waiting. As I examined him more closely, though, my relief waned. He was a small, stout, roughly-shaven man, maybe in his late thirties. The clapped-out motorbike was precariously balanced against the school gate and on the back carrier was a cardboard box, strapped on with a variety of oddments of rope. A few roughly cut air-holes suggested that my patient was lurking inside.

However, I was more concerned about the client. I watched cautiously in the rear-view mirror as he made his way over to me with a slow shuffle. A quick glance confirmed that there was no one else around. His appearance was enhanced by a tattered leather biker's jacket, under which the string vest did little to hide the tattoos that ran in an irregular pattern across his chest. I thought briefly of pretending that I was another client, but the absence of any animal made that excuse seem unlikely.

My client rapped sharply on my car window and I felt it rude not to wind it down a fraction, although the doors remained firmly locked.

'Are you de vet?' he growled in at me, in a menacing voice.

'Em, yeah. That's right,' I replied, cautiously, 'but the clinic's not here yet and I've no drugs or needles or anything ...' I trailed off as I realised how this must have sounded.

'I don't want drugs or nothin' offa ye,' he replied, not seeming to be in the least bit offended. 'I have a patient for ye in de box,' he added.

'Ah, in the box,' I confirmed, as though this was an

unusual situation. 'Well, we'd better not let him out until the mobile clinic gets here,' I added brightly, 'in case he gets a fright or something ...'

'Wadever ye say!' and he paused a moment to eye me speculatively. 'She's probably wettin' 'erself in der, all right,' he added, matter of factly.

Thankfully, at that moment a little old lady arrived with her geriatric Yorkshire Terrier. I decided it would be gallant of me to get out of the car to keep an eye on her.

As my biker swung his leg over the Honda, he kicked the starter and the old bike spluttered into life. The tiny Yorkshire yapped shrilly and her owner let out a yell: 'Will ye turn dat bleedin' racket off, ye big edjit, ye!' I was obviously redundant.

The engine died instantly and my biker client threw a 'Sorry 'bout dat, Missis,' over his shoulder to where the stooped old lady stood, fuming.

Within minutes, the scene was transformed as the pavements filled with every type of pet, adult and child imaginable. Soon afterwards, the mobile clinic arrived, with Gordon driving as usual. I was never brave enough to try to sort out the queue. I usually left that to Eamon, the assistant, who had over forty years' experience at the clinic. Usually the crowd was relatively calm, and he would just open up the doors and called out, 'Who's first, please?', and hope not to start a riot.

Tonight, the little old lady came first. 'That big lout can wait,' she declared as she made her way up the steep steps of the van with the tiny dog hugged tightly to her chest.

Tiny, as she was called, squealed as though she was

being murdered as I clipped each one of her nails, hoping not to raise blood in the black, overgrown claws, under the beady eye of her owner.

'Ah, ye poor little pet,' crooned the owner as the tiny terrier sank one of her rotten teeth into Eamon's cuffs. He held the dog firmly, and I knew I could work in relative safety.

'Is dey hurtin' me poor little luv?' she asked the dog, who was much too busy trying to wrestle her teeth through the thankfully thick material.

Eamon pursed his lips and grinned at me over the shaggy demon while I clipped as fast as I dared before nodding at him to release the patient.

'They should be okay for a good long time now,' I assured the ungrateful old lady as she left without a word.

'I don't know what to make of your man,' I muttered to Eamon as my biker appeared next.

'How are yis!' he said, nodding briefly at Eamon and Gordon before turning to face me.

'She's in der,' he told me, handing me the box.

With tremulous hands, I gingerly untied the loose string, wondering what 'she' was going to be. Mentally, I conjured up an image of a python or two, complete with tattoos and studded collar. Gordon and Eamon watched.

Holding three edges firmly in place, I cautiously peeled open the fourth before peering inside from a safe distance. An expectant hush fell as my eyes became accustomed to the shadowy figure in the furthest corner of the box – the shadowy figure of a small, fluffy rabbit.

I looked from the biker to Eamon, to Gordon, and tried

to suppress a giggle. Eamon and Gordon continued to stare as I reached my hand in to capture the patient. Eamon was holding a pair of protective gloves.

Jed, the biker, finally introduced himself, then he glared menacingly as though daring me to laugh. 'Is it broke or wha'?'

The 'it', I soon realised, referred to the hind leg that hung at an awkward angle from the shivering, furry creature.

Although the answer was obvious, I carefully rotated the ends of the fractured tibia, noticing that the tiny fibula had shattered into multiple fragments, which floated freely underneath the fine skin.

Snake food, was my initial reaction. Obviously, Jed was keeping rabbits to feed his snakes – Jed, the Head, with his studded pythons. But then, why would he be concerned about the broken leg? I felt sorry for the fawnish-brown creature with her floppy ears, but at least I could put her to sleep humanely and put an end to her worries and pain. The fracture itself was a nasty one.

'Yes. I'm afraid it is broken. We'll have to put her to sleep,' I replied firmly, in case he had any notions of taking her home the way she was.

I looked up at him, determined to fight my case, and was totally astounded to see the bulky frame dissolve into a quivering mass as tears started to flow freely down his toughened face.

'Ah Jayney, no!' he wailed, throwing his arms down on the tiny examination table.

The tension was electric, as we all stood, immobilised, not knowing what to make of his reaction.

'Can yez do nuthin' at all for 'er?' he implored, looking up at me.

The tiny rabbit sat quietly in my arms, nose twitching impatiently, totally indifferent to the scene that she had created.

'Well, there is a possibility,' I began slowly, 'that we could refer you to a private clinic and maybe they could do something with it.'

'D'ye tink so?' he asked, suddenly hopeful, but then added with resignation, 'I suppose dat'll cost me a bleedin' stack o' dosh?'

'Well, it certainly won't be cheap,' I confirmed.

'Ah sure, Jayney, I've no bleedin' money.' He dug his hands into the torn leather pocket and pulled out an assortment of coppers and coins, about enough for a Big Mac on the way home.

'Dat's all I have. Been on de labour since I did me back in. Can yez not do nuttin'?'

I glanced outside at the impatient queue and over to our bandage cupboard, stocked to deal with minor injuries only.

Jed looked around at each one of us and made one last desperate attempt: 'Ye see, it's me little girl's rabbi'. Tinks the world of it, she does.' His eyes fixed on mine, as though aware of my hesitation. He knew he had me.

'Well, okay,' I said wearily. 'But there's no guarantee. I'll put a cast on it, but it's an awkward fracture to cast and there are a lot of broken ends. It's only a small chance that it may work,' I said firmly, watching as his eyes took on new hope.

Ignoring the fact that we would be there until well after the appointed clinic time, I ran out to my car to get a roll of plaster of Paris, avoiding the nice fibreglass cast, as there was no electricity in the clinic, essential to operate the cast cutters when the time came to remove a fibreglass cast.

Gordon held the tiny rabbit as I carefully realigned the broken pieces. I could hear Eamon bargaining with the increasingly agitated crowd outside. I concentrated on placing the casting material in such a way that it would not rub the thin, almost hairless skin on the inside of the thigh and yet would support the mush of bones underneath.

'I suppose we'd better call 'er Lucky, now,' declared Jed, clearly delighted with the turn of events.

The cast set almost uneventfully, with only one dodgy moment when 'Lucky' tried to buck out of Gordon's careful restraint, but, thankfully, didn't upset the bandaging. Having double-checked the padding, I sent Jed off with a list of instructions and a dire prognosis.

It seemed a long week until the following Wednesday night when I met Jed for a recheck. Again, we met alone, but this time I got out of the car to check on my patient, who seemed bright and alert, and unperturbed by the great mass of plaster-encumbered leg which dangled awkwardly beneath.

'Have you told your daughter it might not work? Does she know we may still have to put the rabbit to sleep?' I hounded him, not wanting to be responsible for a little girl's heartbreak.

'Ah yeah, she knows dat, an' all,' he assured me before I sent him on his way with an arrangement to see him the following Wednesday.

I tried not to think what was happening underneath the cast, which at least hadn't fallen off yet but was probably concealing a massive wound slough or the beginnings of a gangrenous leg.

When Jed didn't turn up for our rendezvous the following week, or the week after that, I assumed the worst. I berated myself for my poor judgement in prolonging the pain for both the helpless rabbit and the heartbroken child.

I didn't know how to react when I saw the battered Honda the week after, though. Either the rabbit was still alive, or Jed had come looking for trouble.

Miraculously, the rabbit looked well as she poked her dainty head out of the top of the box, obviously becoming accustomed to her regular motorbike rides. The tissue above and below the cast seemed fine and there was no obvious smell, but the cast had slipped a little bit.

'Right,' I said decisively. 'Let's take it off.'

I knew the van wouldn't arrive for at least another fifteen minutes and removing a cast is a notoriously tedious job. Ignoring my better sense, I opened the passenger door of the car and indicated to Jed, 'Right so. Hop in!'

Once inside, despite the unusually sweltering weather, we had to close all the windows in case Lucky, who wasn't quite so manageable in Jed's hands, escaped. The sweat poured down my face and onto the cast as I alternately cut and sawed at the now-grimy material. Soon the front seat was covered in a fine sprinkling of white powder which could have made our meeting look even more suspicious had anyone cared to notice.

With one side cut open, I could wait no longer. I carefully manipulated the length of the limb and there it was – an admittedly large, but nonetheless supporting callus, indicating that the fracure had healed.

'It's looking good,' I said, trying to restrain my enthusiasm as I glanced up at Jed and tried not to laugh at the rapturous smile that lit up his face. 'Still, wait until we get the whole lot of it off,' I cautioned as I carefully peeled the other side off, terrified of re-breaking what would still be a very fragile repair. I gently probed my finger in underneath the other side and was dismayed when I saw the trickle of discharge. I cursed myself for my hopeful prognosis when the tip of my finger ran into a piece of bone, clearly palpable, sticking out though the skin, creating an open wound.

'No! I'm sorry, Jed. It's not as good as I thought. Look you can see the open wound here,' and I pulled off the remaining bandage to reveal a tiny splinter of bone sticking out. But as I examined it, the fragment popped right out, leaving the remaining repair looking almost passable. Clearly, a small fragment had been separated from its blood supply and the healthy tissue had literally spat it out from the otherwise healthy repair.

A quick swab revealed that the remaining tissue was fine and the tiny wound would close over in a matter of days.

'Well, is she knackered or wha'?' asked Jed, anxiously studying my face.

'No. It's okay. I actually think it's going to be okay,' I replied incredulously, carefully manipulating the limb through an admittedly somewhat limited range of motion.

'It's fine. Not a bother on her,' I confirmed, looking with delight at my ecstatic client. 'With a little bit of light exercise the leg will loosen out. You can tell your little girl that Lucky is going to be as good as new.'

There was no time left as already a curious queue had gathered and appeared to be engrossed at the sight of myself and Jed squashed in my little Opel Corsa, behind steamed-up windows. My face was flushed with heat, and sweat poured off me as I hastily grabbed my clinic coat to pull on over my sweat-soaked T-shirt. My little lady from the first night was standing close by, scandalised at the vision.

'A young wan, like yerself!' she retorted, clearly none too pleased.

'Sorry to keep you waiting,' I told her sweetly. 'You see, I just had to take the cast off his daughter's rabbit. The leg was broken but now it's as good as new,' I informed them all, delighted to share the good news.

'Jed's daughter!' she said, her already shrill voice rising a few octaves. 'Sure, that waster lives around the corner from me. Lived dere all 'is life, more's de pity. He don't have no bleedin' daughter,' she told me, enjoying the look of shock on my face. 'Or if he does, it's not one 'e's admittin' to, anyway,' she stated.

CHAPTER THREE

THREE LITTLE GIRLS
AND THEIR DOG

You couldn't but admire the sleek, glossy-coated Golden Retriever that majestically swept into the consulting room. She paused as she came through the doorway and glanced back to check that the three little girls, accompanied by their frazzled-looking mother, were coming with her. Her shaggy face broke into a wide grin as she plonked herself down on the floor beside me and offered an enormous feathered paw.

'My name's Kate and her name's Gemma and she's mine,' explained the youngest of the three. She couldn't have been more than three or four years old.

'Is not,' retorted the next one up, about fifteen centimetres taller. 'She's mine.'

'She's all of ours, isn't that right, Mammy?' demanded the

eldest, obviously the peacemaker in the family.

'That's right, Sarah. Now, girls, keep quiet or you'll have to wait outside.'

'Would you like to bring your sisters to see a rabbit?' I asked, addressing Sarah.

An excited babble broke out as I called Melissa from the office to take them out the back where a large and friendly rabbit resided. I felt this was the easiest way to keep them quiet.

'Thanks a million!' said Teresa, their mother. 'They have me driven mad all morning.'

'Don't worry. That rabbit is worth his weight in gold for this sort of job. He'll keep them occupied for as long as we need. What's wrong with Gemma?'

'It's probably nothing, but when we got up this morning, there was some vomit on the floor. She didn't eat her breakfast and she's normally such a glutton. '

'Right, let's have a look at her,' I replied, hauling the gentle giant up onto the consulting table.

Gemma responded with a steady thump of her tail as I examined her. Everything seemed to be in perfect order, apart from a slight tenderness in her abdomen.

'Any chance she could have got at the dustbin or eaten any of the kids' toys?' I inquired as I continued to palpate the abdomen, trying to pinpoint any specific area of tenderness.

'Well, she's like a dustbin herself. She'd eat anything, but I don't think I left any bins out. We're very careful with her. She has chewed a few of the girls' toys before, but that was when she was a puppy.'

'When did she last pass any droppings or would you have noticed?'

Teresa thought for a moment. 'I'm not sure, to be honest. She usually goes down in the bushes at the end of the garden, so I wouldn't really know.'

'Not to worry. She's probably just eaten something that didn't agree with her. Her temperature is normal and she seems very bright. I'll give her an injection to stop her vomiting and a muscle relaxant. Don't give her anything to eat for the rest of the day but let her drink as much of this as she wants,' I added, handing her a couple of sachets of electrolyte mix.

As though on cue, the three girls trooped back in.

'His name's Roger an' his ears are 'normous,' announced Kate.

The middle child tugged gently at her mother's hand. 'Please, Mammy, could we have him? He's really cute and I think he likes me.'

'Now, Mary,' began Teresa, looking at me in horror.

'No, girls. I'm afraid Roger has to stay here. But you can come and visit him whenever you want,' I added, seeing a few tears threatening to brim over.

Teresa shot me a grateful look.

'Did Gemma eat any of your toys recently?' I began, rapidly changing the subject.

'Yeah, she did. She ate my Barbie's arm and she chewed the ear off my Furby,' replied Kate, indignantly, hands on hips.

'Yes, love, but that was over a year ago,' reminded Teresa gently.

'I know that,' she replied scornfully, 'but still, I haven't forgotten, have I, Gemma?' She shook an admonitory finger at the big dog who didn't even have the good grace to look remotely guilty.

'I'm going to give her an injection now to make her better and then you can take her home with you, but I don't want any of you playing with her today and if you do, make sure you wash your hands afterwards.'

'It's purely a precaution,' I reassured Teresa, 'but you can't be too careful with kids just in case there is any infection there.'

'I think I'm going to be sick,' came a quiet wail from the corner.

'Now, Mary, don't worry. I know you hate injections.'

'Would a sweet help?' I offered, holding out a jar that proved to be just as invaluable as Roger.

The jar disappeared out my hands as quick as lightning.

Sarah came up to Gemma as I drew up the medication from a vial into the syringe. 'Don't worry. I'll hold your paw for you.'

Gemma braced herself in rigid martyrdom as I gently injected the clear liquid under the skin. 'I think there's a bit of the old soldier going on here,' I said. 'You've that much fat under there you couldn't possibly have felt a thing.'

Gemma grinned apologetically as I patted her head. Once I had finished with her, she hopped eagerly down off the table with the agility of an animal that looked far from ill.

'Now, take her home and look after her,' I said, handing the lead to Sarah.

They trooped out the door, dutifully chorusing their 'thank yous'.

'Let me know how she is tomorrow.'

'I will of course. And thank you so much.'

I didn't think any further about Gemma and her lively comrades until the phone rang in the surgery the next morning.

'A Teresa Kenny on the phone for you,' said Melissa.

'Teresa, how are you?' I asked, picking up the phone in the consulting room. 'And more to the point, how's Gemma?'

'Oh I'm fine thanks – well, nothing a good night's sleep wouldn't sort out. I'm not so sure about Gemma, though.'

I was surprised. I had expected that her recovery would have been trouble free.

'I didn't give her any food at all yesterday, although she kept following me every time I went into the kitchen. She wasn't sick either. But then I gave her a little bit of chicken and rice, like you said.'

'And did she eat that?' I asked.

'Oh she did. She wolfed it down. She must have been starving, but about an hour later she got sick again.'

'And did you notice if she passed any droppings or not?'

'I kept her in the house all day, so I'm positive that she hasn't, but still, she hasn't eaten, so I suppose that's normal, is it?' she asked hopefully.

'Well, it may be, but I'd still rather she'd passed something. How is she in herself? Does she seem to be in good form?'

'Oh, she's in great form; still playing with the kids all day. Kate spent the morning trying to ride her up and down the hall,' exclaimed Teresa.

'Poor Gemma,' I laughed. 'It's probably nothing serious but I think you should let me have another look at her, just in case. I know you have your hands full, but do you think you could get her down to me?'

'Of course. That's no problem. I'd be happier myself if you saw her. I don't think I could face the kids if anything happened to her.'

'You'd never be forgiven.'

'There's just one other thing. We're going away camping for the weekend. We're leaving tomorrow morning. Do you think she'll be okay by then?'

'I hope so, but don't worry. We'll sort something out if she isn't fit to travel. We can always keep her in for the weekend if necessary.'

'Oh could you? That would be great, thanks. The kids have been really looking forward to the trip. I'll get down to you before lunch anyway.'

When Gemma arrived, she looked as magnificent as ever. After sending the girls off to check on Roger for me, I knelt down on the floor beside her and again palpated the abdomen; it was no better or no worse than the day before. Her temperature was still normal.

'You're quite sure she hasn't passed anything since I saw her last? That would worry me a bit.'

'No, there's no way she could have. I brought her out into the garden on a lead a few times and she did a few wees all right, but nothing else. Why, what are you thinking of?'

'Well, with her still vomiting, it's possible that she may

have an obstruction in her gut. I can't feel anything very obvious, but she is a little bit tender.'

Teresa's face paled with anxiety. 'That would be serious, wouldn't it?'

'Well, to be honest, it could be,' I said. 'It depends on what's causing it. Quite often big dogs like Gemma manage to pass all sorts of things without too much trouble.'

'I really don't think she could have got at anything. Frank, my husband, and I went through everything last night. There was nothing left lying around.'

'Well, let's hope for the best. I'm going to continue on with her other medication and I'll give her an antibiotic, just in case. I also want you to give her this liquid paraffin at home. Just keep her somewhere that you can clean easily. Sometimes it can make a bit of a mess,' I warned her.

'Oh, I wouldn't care. Once Gemma's all right.'

I went to call the girls back. They had gone suspiciously quiet. All three stood in the doorway looking innocently at me. There was no sign of Roger.

'Where is he?' I asked.

'Nowhere,' they replied in unison, gazing angelically at me. I was puzzled until I noticed a slight movement in the pink Barbie bag that appeared to be weighing Kate down. Laughing at their inventiveness, I aborted the kidnap mission, returning the indignant Roger to his hutch.

'I don't know what she'll get up to next,' said Teresa, raising her eyes to heaven.

I hoped not to hear any more from them but, on the dot of nine the next morning, Teresa was waiting at the front door with Gemma.

'I left the kids at home packing with Frank. I'm getting really worried about Gemma,' she blurted out.

Although still standing proudly, Gemma did look a bit subdued.

'She still hasn't passed anything,' she said, anticipating my next question. 'Most of the time, she's in good form, but yesterday evening, I thought she was very quiet in herself. Sarah won't leave her side. She says she doesn't want to go away without her.'

As before, there was no temperature and despite my deep probing, Gemma didn't appear to be unduly painful; only a slight flinching of the muscle indicated any potential problem. If you didn't know her, you wouldn't have noticed there was anything wrong with her at all.

'Is she still vomiting?' I asked Teresa, when I had completed my examination.

'There was a little bit on the floor this morning, but not as much as before.'

'And is she drinking a lot?'

'She's drinking the electrolyte, all right, but I wouldn't say any more than usual.'

'What I'd really love to do is to take some radiographs,' I confided in Teresa, 'but our x-ray machine has been giving problems and has been taken away to be serviced. We won't have it back for at least two weeks. It's probably best if I refer you to one of the other practices. I'm sure they'd be happy to take her.'

Teresa didn't hesitate as she shook her head. 'Thanks, but no. I'd rather you dealt with her yourself.'

Although I was pleased with her confidence in me, I

might have been more relieved if she had taken me up on the offer.

'Do you think you'll have to operate on her? I'm terrified she might not survive. I know the kids won't want to go away if they hear she's having an operation. We've been looking forward to this holiday for so long.'

I could well believe her. With her pale complexion and the bags under her eyes, she looked like she could do with a break, although I wasn't sure if camping with the lively trio would be much of a rest.

I hesitated. 'Let's give her one more day. Without a radiograph, our only option is to do an exploratory laparotomy, to actually open her up and see what's going on. But it's a big operation to put her through and she's not really sick enough to justify that at this stage.'

Teresa looked relieved. 'Whatever you think is best yourself.'

'Just go off and try to enjoy yourselves. We'll keep her in for the weekend and I'll let you know how she's getting on. Just leave me your mobile number.'

Teresa quietly shed a few tears as she said goodbye. I couldn't help wondering if I was doing the right thing.

Melissa, the nurse, came in, laughing, a few hours later. 'Look what just came in the letter box.'

It was an enormous card in childish handwriting address to 'Ms Gemma Kenny'. 'We love you, Gemma. Get well soon,' it read. Sarah, Mary and Kate had scrawled their names at the bottom; Kate, by joining the dots. It scared me to think how much this dog meant to them.

We gave Gemma a stronger dose of liquid paraffin and

an enema and I repeated the powerful muscle relaxing injection before settling her down for the evening. I prepared a surgical kit and placed it in the autoclave, hoping that it wouldn't be required. She seemed to be in good form when I left her but I lay awake, tossing and turning throughout the night. Mad dreams of Furbys and Barbie dolls, squashed in the delicate intestine, interrupted my sleep and I repeatedly woke up in a sweat. I was glad when the dawn broke.

The next morning, I went in early. I hoped I would find copious amounts of faeces but all that was there was some frothy vomit. I knew I could put it off no longer. Reluctantly, I rang Teresa.

'I'm sorry, Teresa, but I'll have to go ahead and operate. I don't want to let her go on any longer.'

There was a silence as Teresa tried to control the wobble in her voice. 'I'm really sorry to put you to this trouble, especially on a Sunday, but whatever you think is best.'

'I'll ring as soon as I'm finished. Try not to worry,' I reassured her. If only I could follow my own advice.

Although sedated, Gemma thumped her tail softly as I injected the anaesthetic into her vein. Her head slumped on the table as the drug took effect. Soon she lay, clipped and prepped, under the green surgical drapes. I couldn't help but imagine the faces of three anxious little girls as I sliced into the smooth skin. Thick wads of fat covered the midline and had to be separated before I could incise into the abdomen. At least now I would know what exactly the problem was.

I stared in disbelief as I examined the coils of intestine; the colour ranged from healthy pink to congested red, to purple and, in parts, to the blackish colour that every vet dreads. As I carefully manipulated the loops of inflamed tissue, I could get an impression of a hard, irregular substance filling several sections of gut. In between, the loops were bloated with gas. I was well aware of the correct technique of 'milking' the foreign body to a piece of healthy intestine and incising into that loop to remove the offending article. But in this case, it wasn't possible as the obstruction was in not one but several portions of the intestine and seemed to be well trapped in the thickened muscular rings.

Starting with the biggest section, I cut through the muscle wall and could feel the sharp point of the scalpel blade scrape off a metal-like substance. Picking up a forceps, I grasped the edge of the foreign body and tried to ease out the irregular, elongated mass. I winced as the sharp edges snagged the delicate lining of the gut. Having pulled out a piece approximately ten centimetres long, I unravelled it to find out what it was: the shredded remains of a Chinese takeaway container. If this had been the only section of the gut to be damaged, I could have just removed the damaged necrotic section and rejoined the healthy ends, but it was nowhere near that simple. Gently, I manipulated the next portion of damaged gut out of the abdomen and carried on easing out loop after loop of intestine, in varying degrees of necrosis. By the time it was all spread out over the sterile laparotomy sponges, it was clear that there was precious little healthy intestine left. I wondered how on earth Gemma could have looked so well and shown so few clinical signs with the extensive damage inside.

Without remembering the exact detail, I could recall a study from college days where dogs had survived with large portions of their intestine removed. However, the damage to Gemma's intestine was so extensive that I wasn't confident that she could survive if I were to remove it all in one piece. My only alternative was to remove each section separately. I began the painstaking job of repairing the damaged gut as best I could. I struggled trying to decide which pieces to remove and which to retain. I sweated as I made long incisions into the damaged tissue, as there was no way I could pull out the metallic container without tearing the gut. I vaguely remembered from my surgical lectures how an incision should never be more than ... was it one and a half times the diameter of the gut?

My fingers ached as I rejoined lengths of gut where I had had to remove a dead section. It seemed to take hours as I fiddled with the tiny lengths of suture material. My back ached and my eyes were blurring by the time I had finally finished. I flushed large volumes of warmed saline through the abdomen, hoping to remove any intestinal fluid that might have leaked out. With the last syringeful, I added some soluble antibiotic. Carefully, I wrapped all the repaired sections in the glistening omentum, the supportive sling that cradles the internal organs. I hoped it would do its job and soak up any leakage from the rejoined sections. Soon, all that remained visible of my work was a neat row of sutures in the skin. I shuddered to think of the horrors that lay hidden beneath.

While waiting for Gemma to wake up, I rang Teresa. The phone was answered on the first ring. I recognised the babyish tones of Kate.

'Is my dog better now? Mummy told me you're going to cut out the bad bits.'

'Gillian, I'm sorry about that.' Teresa sounded flustered. 'How is she?'

I paused. 'I'm sorry, Teresa, but it's not looking good.' As painlessly as I knew how, I explained my worries.

Teresa couldn't hold back the tears as I told her what the culprit was and she remembered. 'We had a Chinese on Wednesday night. When the container was gone the next morning, I assumed Frank had thrown it out. I should have known better. How could I be so stupid? It's just the sort of thing she'd go for.'

'Don't blame yourself,' I consoled her. 'It can happen so easily. But right now it's up to Gemma. She's a strong dog. She may just pull through. I'll let you know how she is tonight.'

'Of course, and listen, thanks so much for everything. You sound absolutely exhausted.'

I sincerely hoped she would have something to thank me for. A niggling doubt in my mind kept asking if I should have operated sooner.

By Tuesday night when the Kennys returned, Gemma was ready to go home. I had been in touch with them a few times a day and I had reassured them that everything was going as well as could be expected. Despite my cautious warnings, Teresa became more enthusiastic with every passing hour.

'I just know she'll pull through,' she kept saying.

I didn't like to put a damper on her hopes, but I couldn't forget the mess of intestine beneath the neat row of stitches.

When Teresa and the gang arrived to collect Gemma, the enormous bouquet of flowers almost hid the three small girls as Sarah and Kate struggled to carry them. Mary brought up the rear with a card not unlike the one Gemma had got.

'We love you. Thank you for making our dog better. From Sarah, Mary and Kate.'

While thanking them profusely, I cautioned Teresa. 'It's not all over yet. It takes at least five days for the wound to heal. There's an awful lot of damage inside.'

'I know, but just look at her. She looks so well.'

I said nothing but hoped, as I had never hoped before, that my doubts were mislaid.

I heard nothing for two days.

I was just beginning to relax when on Friday morning, I opened the waiting room door to see Teresa, Gemma and the girls inside. I quickly ushered the kids off to Roger with the promise of a lollipop if they didn't try to kidnap him.

'She's been in absolutely brilliant form, better than ever before. But she didn't eat very well this morning. I thought you'd like to see her.'

I cursed to myself as I read her temperature. One hundred and three. This was just what I had been dreading. Gemma winced as I palpated her abdomen. I could just imagine the contaminating fluids leaking from the sieve-like gut into the abdomen, and the resultant peritonitis. I shook my head slowly at Teresa.

'This is what I was afraid of. We'll have to keep her in again.'

The lollipops consoled the three girls enormously when I explained to them that Gemma would have to stay with me again.

'She must like you an awful lot,' said Kate nodding her head wisely.

I hoped they would still like me when this was over.

I rang an older and more experienced colleague to look for advice.

'Should I try opening her up again?'

'Good Lord, no. There's nothing more you can do than what you're doing already. By the sounds of it, the whole thing was a disaster from the start. I think you'll lose her, but still, you never know ...'

I wished I hadn't rung him.

I seemed to spend the next three days either with Gemma or on the phone to Teresa. Gemma was getting steadily worse.

'If she's no better by tomorrow, we'll have to start thinking if it's fair to let her go on much longer,' I said quietly to Teresa.

She wasn't able to answer me.

The next morning, Gemma was dead.

I couldn't believe it as I stared at what remained of the once majestic animal, the 'big sister' to three bright and happy young girls.

I broke down when I rang Teresa to tell her.

'I'm so sorry,' I said, so aware of the inadequacy of the words.

I never saw Teresa or her three little girls again. I don't know if they ever got another dog or if they had lost faith in me – either way, I couldn't blame them.

CHAPTER FOUR

A HELPING HAND

I am fully convinced that to the day I die I will be absolutely useless at dehorning cattle. From the time I first qualified, it seemed that the simple act of detaching cattle from their horns was not for me. After a few hopeless attempts high up in the Dublin mountains during my first year in practice, I wasn't too concerned at my seeming lack of natural aptitude for the job – after all, at the time I didn't seem to have a natural aptitude for anything veterinary related! But, as time passed, I gradually found myself becoming less useless at certain jobs, and on certain occasions I really thought I was becoming in some way competent. But with dehorning cattle – or 'skulling' as it was known – I seemed to make little progress. Within a short time, I became proficient at injecting the local anaesthetic to numb the nerve supply to the horn. I enjoyed carefully inserting the needle in under the ridge of bone knowing that any further resentment on the part of the animal would be purely due to being handled and not due to any pain. After that, however, everything would start to go wrong. For a whole month I used nothing but the crange – a large metal guillotine-type instrument. Strong yearlings and two-week old calves alike, I towered over them brandishing the huge blades and, yes, it did work fine on the small calves, apart from a slight difficulty in balancing the enormous instrument on the 3cm-long stumps that would one day become horns. Meanwhile, anything with a decent-sized blood vessel would bleed profusely the instant the heavy blades met.

'It's the angle you have wrong,' assured one of the vets I had seen practice with. 'Get it at more of a slope and you won't get bleeders.'

But, no. I still got bleeders.

'You want to get further down the horn, right in tight to the skull,' said another. 'But be careful,' he added, 'I remember once I went too tight and I cracked her skull. She ended up in the factory.'

So then I tried the embryotomy wire – a heavy-duty, sharpened metal wire attached to two metal handles which was looped around the base of the horn, allowing the horn to be sawn off. Apart from the fact that every time I dehorned a beast it was like having a work-out in the gym, I thought I was getting there. Yes, they still bled a little bit, but it didn't look quite so gruesome. However, one particularly hardy bullock destroyed my progress. The first horn was tough going and my face went from various shades of pink to red, to beetroot, to purple as I valiantly sawed, thrashing around in unison with the furious animal, but eventually the offending horn did drop to the ground. Resisting the urge to retch, I flopped at the side of the crush until the shaking in my shoulders and wrists had subsided enough to have a go at the second side. Off I went again, sawing and sawing, but the more I went on, the less progress I seemed to make. Back and forth I sawed, until the wire stopped, trapped deep in the horny tissue. With a bit of assistance from the farmer, who seemed sympathetic enough to my plight, I managed to release the wire as he pushed against the cut edge of the horn. Only a few strokes in, the same thing happened, but this time nothing would budge the wire. It was as though the heat created by the burning had welded the wire into the horn.

Too exhausted to be embarrassed, I went back to the jeep to get the crange to finish off the job. The temptation to drive away and never come back was almost irresistible. As the wire was wedged in the horn just exactly where I wanted to place the crange, I knew that this was going to be yet another botched job. The torrents of blood that shot out at all angles as soon as I had cut off the offending horn was like none before, and despite my best efforts, poking and prodding with a forceps, the unfortunate beast was still bleeding heavily by the time I had finished. I wearily picked up a strand of baling twine and tied it tightly around the base where the horn had once been, until the bleeding stopped. It would have looked absurd enough, but with the length of wire still firmly wedged at the base of the horn it looked ludicrous. The twine was removed the next day by the farmer and the bullock suffered no ill-effects, but to this day, if he is still alive, that strand of wire is still stuck in the remnant of his horn.

By this time, I was into my next season and some of the farmers were ringing to complain that some of the ones I had dehorned the previous season had started to grow horns back again as my cautious nipping off of the top did not remove the base of the growing horn.

Now I changed tack and, having given up on my own skills, I tried the animal welfare issue. No sooner would a calf I had safely delivered drop to the floor than I would begin a lengthy lecture to the farmer on the merits of early debudding: by burning the developing bud of horn at a young age any further horn growth would be prevented.

'You can't beat it,' I would plead with them. 'Do it now and it will save all the hassle and expense later on. You won't believe how much they will thrive,' I would plead. 'You won't set them back at all in the autumn time.'

Farmers that I would meet in passing at the local mart or in the co-op would equally be awarded one of my lectures. I was convinced I had gone too far, however, when after a tough caesarean at three o'clock one morning, I earnestly delivered my speech to the bewildered farmer, who was obviously too polite to point out that the calf was a polled breed and never would grown horns anyway!

My final solution was to avoid the issue at all costs. It was amazing the excuses you could come up with if you tried hard enough. It was incredible how often the blades in the crange had broken that very morning or I had just used up my last bit of embryotomy wire on a difficult calving.

'Sure, not to worry,' the farmer would say good-naturedly, 'you can do them when you come back in three days' time to read the test.'

When a call was booked specifically to dehorn, I would bargain with whichever other vet I was working with at the time.

'Okay so, you dehorn the two bullocks and I'll do your evening clinic for you tonight,' I would offer, knowing that an hour and a half-long clinic would be easier. I got very ingenious, but I couldn't get away with it forever.

*   *   *

I was right at the top of the Sally Gap one fateful day when I got the dreaded message – three to be dehorned in Laragh. As I was the only vet on call that day, it had to be me and I had been through every excuse in the book.

'Listen, James,' I said to the farmer on the phone, having introduced myself, 'about those bullocks you have for dehorning today, it's no problem at all to do them, but it's just that I'm on my own today and I have a lot of calls in and it's very busy, so is there any chance we could leave them till next week?' I ended lamely before I started to gabble too much.

'Sorry, Gillian, and I know I left it late, but we had a bit of trouble at home here – one of the chaps was sick in hospital. Those bullocks are due to go to the mart next week so I really need to get them done today.'

There was nothing for it; it would have to be done. As I pulled up to the yard, I noticed that it was actually a car-repair garage with a small bit of land attached. They were obviously part-time farmers, which did nothing for my impending sense of doom as I knew it meant that the handling facilities were less likely to be adequate.

Having prepared my syringes of local anaesthetic and the antibiotic powder, I pulled on the well-worn, well-washed overalls that I reserved specifically for skulling cattle.

It'll be fine, I assured myself calmly as I made my way up to the garage. Just three small weanlings. I'll be done in no time. I tried to remind myself of all the successful dehornings I had done in the past. That didn't take long.

I called out around the yard, but could find no-one. The shed was empty, apart from three enormous well-horned beasts, penned in the corner.

Ah no, I thought to myself, it couldn't be them.

It was. I couldn't believe that these three cattle, with mature horns as thick as miniature tree trunks, were to be my patients for the morning.

As I shouted into the garage, a young lad came out looking none too pleased to be disturbed.

'Is James around at all?' I asked, courteously.

'No, he had to go off,' he replied curtly, before turning away to resume his work.

'Well, I'm here to dehorn the cattle,' I replied, trailing lamely after him.

'They're in the pen for you,' he told me, without raising his head. 'Work away.'

My patience was beginning to fade. 'Well, I'll need help with it. If not, it'll just have to be done another day.'

'He said he needs them done today but he had to go out,' he answered, without enthusiasm, dashing all my hopes.

'Okay,' I said, resignedly facing the inevitable. 'But, I'll need you to help, so.'

You wouldn't have died of excitement with the mono-syllabic conversation that followed between us. I just about got out of him that his name was Declan and that he lived in Dun Laoghaire. The nearest he had come to cattle, until now, was looking out the window of the garage where he was serving his apprenticeship. In his favour, he was at least six feet tall and looked as though he worked out most nights of the week. I carefully injected the local anaesthetic under the rim of bone that covered the nerve supply while he held determinedly onto the metal tongs as the bullock tried in vain to whip his head away. As I worked under Declan's scornful gaze, I was relieved that, so far, everything seemed to going quite smoothly, consid-ering the odds. Having waited a few minutes for the local anaesthetic to take effect, it came to the part where I placed the blades of the crange around the enormous horns. I gradually pulled the handles open as far as I could, but this came nowhere near wide enough to get anywhere near the base of the horn. I pulled again and although I managed to open them a centimetre or two wider, it was still nowhere near wide enough to do the job.

Eventually, still trying to appear calm and in control, I jumped down off the crush and had to stand on one handle and pull with all my might to open up the blade until the handles were at a one hundred and eighty degree angle. With the instrument locked open at full stretch, I just about managed to pull the blades down to the base of the over-sized horn at an angle that I hoped would do the job.

By this stage, Declan was looking totally bored with the whole process and glanced repeatedly at his watch while muttering to himself and shuffling his feet in the mucky gravel.

Grasping the handles of the crange in my hands with my arms at full stretch, I attempted to close the enormous jaws as the bullock stood, happily ignorant of the entire proceedings. But with the handles locked open, try and try as I did, nothing happened. No matter what angle I pulled from, nothing budged and I came to the realisation that, yet again, I was making a total mess of the job. Declan's bored expression did nothing to encourage me, but I knew that without help I was going nowhere.

'Would you mind,' I began as humbly as I could under the circumstances, 'giving me a bit of a hand closing this?'

'You want *me* to help?' he asked incredulously.

'Yes, if you wouldn't mind,' I laughed, as casually as I could. 'You see, the horns are really very big and it's perfectly normal to need a bit of help with this sort of thing ...'

I stopped abruptly, looking at the disbelief in his face.

'What exactly do you want me to do?' he asked ungraciously.

'Well, if you could just help me close the handles,' I replied, hopping down from my perch and deftly tying a rope halter over the bullock's head and attaching it to the crush before Declan could change his mind.

'You want me to cut them off, you mean?'

'Well, no, not exactly,' I replied as he raised his eyes to heaven. 'If you just pull one handle and I'll pull the other.'

'Oh, get down out of there and I'll do it,' he told me, sighing deeply.

Burning with shame, I stepped down, balancing the crange on the horn until he was ready to take it.

'Just push it down a bit further,' I called to him as he readied himself to cut, trying to restore some control to the situation.

'Do it yourself if you want to,' he retorted, silencing me.

I said nothing as he grasped both handles, one in either hand and tried to close the vast jaws. Taking a deep breath, he clenched his muscled and heaved and heaved, but nothing happened.

I had mixed feelings as I was secretly delighted that he couldn't do it either, but on the other hand I would gladly have been humiliated if it would have put an end to the job.

'Are you sure this is how you're meant to do it? Have you ever even done this before?' he asked as he stopped to catch his breath.

'Oh course!' I replied hastily. 'It's just that James has left them go on too long. In fact, you're really meant to do them at a few weeks old,' I replied, but stopped myself from launching into my usual lecture, which I felt would be wasted under the circumstances.

'Well, they're not going to budge,' he said, puffing slightly after another failed attempt.

'We'll just have to try together,' I decided, jumping up on the crush and grabbing the near handle from Declan, ignoring his obvious misgivings.

'Right now, pull,' I roared as, shoulder to shoulder, we

jostled above the thankfully placid bullock who must have been wondering what exactly we were up to.

'Okay, once more,' I pleaded, after a few vain attempts. This time, just as I felt my eyes were about to pop out and my lungs explode, I could feel a budge and with a dull creaking sound the handles began to creep together.

'Yes, we're getting there!' I cried in triumph to Declan, who returned a withering gaze.

'Go again!' I said with renewed enthusiasm and this time the blades, with a last heave, crashed together with a mighty creak. As the giant horn fell to the ground, so did myself and Declan, unbalanced by the sudden lack of resistance.

As I lay sprawled in his arms in the mucky yard, the laughter that threatened to bubble out at the absurdity of the situation was quickly quelled by the horrified look on my companion's face. I jumped up and calmly continued as though nothing untoward had happened. The fact that half a dozen jets of bright red blood shot out over us did nothing to help the situation, and I fumbled with the forceps, trying desperately to seal off the vessels before we literally painted the shed red.

'Right so, let's get on with the next one,' I encouraged him, having satisfied myself with the first horn.

With difficulty, we repeated the double act, but this time when the horn finally submitted, he jumped clear of the crush just in time to avoid a repeat performance.

The second bullock, although not quite as bad, still required our double force and each time the horn gave, Declan jumped well clear of me as though hit by an electric fence.

The third one, although a hefty animal, I managed on my own, finding an unknown energy force in an attempt to restore even a small fragment of my shattered dignity.

The sheer effort of the work dimmed my embarrassment and by the time I was finishing the last bullock, I was beginning to see the funny side of the situation. Declan, however, still seemed to be in shock.

As I liberally dusted powder on the last horn stump, I heard a jeep pulling up and a man, whom I assumed to be James, stopped beside us. He stared wordless at the three powdered cattle, the vast splashes of red and the stunned look on Declan's face before turning to me.

'You must be James,' I said, extending my bloodstained hand, cheerful now that the job was over.

'And you must be Gillian,' he answered slowly, carefully surveying the scene. 'I'd heard that you are a dab hand at skulling, all right!'

I decided that a rapid exit was the best approach and so I packed away my gear and left the bewildered Declan as he hosed down the walls to rid the shed of the worst of the evidence. As I made my goodbyes, he studiously avoided me, keeping his eyes firmly fixed on the floor.

'Thanks so, Declan,' I called out to him as I left. 'If I ever need a hand again, I'll know where to find you,' and off I went not bothering to wait for a reply that I knew would not be forthcoming.

CHAPTER FIVE

OUT OF THE
HORSE'S MOUTH

Yet again, it was the fancy brochures that attracted my attention. In my early student days, I had been lured by a glossy equivalent to spend two weeks 'seeing practice' in a renowned equine hospital. That fortnight almost put me off the equine side of veterinary practice for life. In both the mixed and small-animal clinics where I had seen practice as a student vet, I had become an integral part of the practice. During my equine practice, however, I was launched into an atmosphere where I competed only with the yard rat in terms of general lowliness. It was a bit of an eye-opener. When I finally qualified, I stayed well away from the equine end of things but, once out in general practice, I was thrown a good measure of horse work, nonetheless. To my delight, I found that despite my lowly status, these equines responded, generally, in the same manner to the usual array of treatment and medications as their bovine and ovine counterparts. Despite not having the appropriate accent, clothing or string of ponies and display of rosettes, it seemed as though the horses themselves, as yet, had not discovered that I was a fraud.

At Riverside Veterinary Clinic we dealt with the usual mix of coughs and colics, vettings and lameness and otherwise routine work. Anything more exciting tended to be referred to the bigger equine hospitals, most of which were centred around Kildare and the hallowed lands of the Curragh.

The glossy brochure that arrived in the office one Friday morning, almost three years into my stay in Riverside, caught my eye almost immediately. It seemed that, despite myself, I still had a vague, if foolish, hope that I could aspire to becoming a competent equine practitioner.

'What do you think of this?' I asked Seamus, my boss, casually, as he came through the office door that morning.

'Well, if I knew what it was I'd have a better idea,' came his cautious reply, obviously sensing that I had a plan on board.

'Equine CPD,' I announced – the CPD standing for Continued Practice Development or, more simply, a course to keep up to date with the latest procedures and treatments. 'An equine course consisting of five modules, to be held over three days and one weekend, encompassing the most popular aspects of equine medicine and surgery,' I quoted towards his retreating back.

'So, what do you think?' I asked again as he returned, brandishing a burdizzo.

'I think you'd be better off spending your time doing a bit of work than hobnobbing with that crowd,' he replied, promptly ending my daydreams of a newly renovated practice, complete with theatre facilities and knock-down boxes and …

By lunchtime, I had tested two hundred cattle, delivered a few lambs and had all but forgotten my noble aspirations. My downfall came in the afternoon when I got a call to a newborn foal. The picture was perfect. A pristine mare, up to her hocks in fresh, golden straw, nuzzling gently at her newborn foal … until I took a closer look. The oversized ears appeared comically long and the almost jelly-like hooves added to the impression that the foal was premature.

'We had her down as being covered on the twelfth of May, but then maybe that was Dancer,' said Darragh, the mare's owner when I enquire as to the foal's due date. 'If that was Dancer,' she continued, that would mean Muffin shouldn't be due for another two weeks.'

Looking at the foal's gaunt body and the deep hollow in her abdomen, I found it hard to believe that she had sucked normally at birth. The ears, sticking out like handlebars, flopped uselessly to one side when I tried to raise the delicate body to a sternal position.

A blood sample would confirm whether the foal had consumed sufficient colostrums, or first milk, to give her a chance to fight the infections that she would encounter over the next few days. As I watched the deep red blood squirting into the sample bottle, I knew that by the time I got the results back from the laboratory, the foal would probably be beyond hope. Regardless, I headed back to the jeep to get the flaskful of colostrum that I had taken from the freezer back at the surgery. It was only with difficulty that I was able to pass a stomach tube down the left nostril and into the foal's empty stomach. It took a couple of attempts and lots of lubricant gel before I was successful. Half an hour later, although now with a full stomach, propped up nicely with a bale of straw, with her long limbs warmly bandaged and under a heat lamp for extra warmth, the foal's chances were realistically not much brighter. The listless eye and drooping head worried me, along with my limited knowledge and equipment to deal with a seriously ill foal. My frustration brought me back to the brochure still lying on office desk.

Back at the surgery later that evening, I rummaged through the pile of papers and, yes, there it was – module five: a detailed review of the common foal illnesses, to include the premature foal, the septic foal and critical care management of the neonate.

I toyed with the idea over the weekend, discussing it with Donal, my husband, who, in fairness, was a lot more enthusiastic than Seamus had been. 'Sure, it's not that far away – you could commute for the weekend if you wanted to. We'd be fine on our own for a bit, wouldn't we, Molly?' he asked her, looking over to where she sat, absorbed in the glossy brochure. 'Robo,' she declared, pointing at the bay horse in the brochure, who to her must have looked like her own bay pony that she had first 'ridden' in her Babygros, although the relative price difference might have involved quite a few decimal points. 'Horsey broken,' she observed on the next page as a flashy-looking chest-nut lay, mid-operation, on a snazzy-looking theatre table. 'Mammy fix'm?' she enquired, looking up at me with the absolute faith of a two-year-old.

I weighed up the pros and cons over the weekend, but by Monday morning I still hadn't come to a decision. It wasn't just the cost that deterred me or even the time away from the practice, as, hopefully, the practice would ulti-mately benefit. Deep in my subconscious was the memory of those appalling two weeks I had spent in the company of some of the most highly-esteemed equine surgeons. What chance would I have with people like that? Or maybe there would be a couple of ordinary vets like myself there too? But what if I made a show of myself with my basic knowledge and equipment? Our stocks of equine medicines weren't exactly state of the art either. Would I end up just displaying my total ignorance?

While I continued to agonise, I was interrupted by the arrival of Arthur, my fellow assistant, who had four years' more experience than I had. His usual jaunty step was noticeably absent.

'Bad weekend?' I enquired sympathetically. He had been on duty.

'One the worst,' he groaned. 'Two caesareans on Satur-day night, a cow with a torsion on Sunday and I was up and down to the Delaney foal all weekend.'

'So, how is the foal, then?' I asked as soon as I could break into his litany of disasters.

'She died last night. I was dripping her and stomach-tubing her all weekend, but she was just a non-runner.'

He carried on with the outcome of a second caesarian but I wasn't listening anymore. Although the foal had died while I was off-duty, I still felt as though it was my case and therefore my fault.

'That's it. I'm doing it,' I decided and before I could change my mind, I filled out the form and hurriedly signed the cheque, trying not to think of the consequences on my monthly bank statement.

Spring passed with a variety of cases – some good, some bad, some downright disastrous. With every equine case I treated, I became increasingly hopeful. Next spring, I'll be ready, I thought to myself.

The first module of the course wasn't until the start of September but it seemed no time at all before the day dawned. The event was to be held in one of the most prestigious hotels in County Kildare – a country manor, steeped in the tradition of all things equine.

Registration and coffee were scheduled for eight-thirty the next morning, so I planned to leave before seven. The night before, as though knowing that something unusual was going on, Molly's normally peaceful bedtime routine ended in tears and I ended up lying crouched in the corner of her cot for over an hour before she reluctantly fell into a restless sleep. She woke several times during the night as though to check if I had left.

The next morning, I was up early and having quickly showered, I dressed myself in what I felt was suitable for the occasion. I strapped Molly into her highchair to feed her with her usual favourite of porridge and apple, but she was having none of it. What didn't hit the far wall or slop down the side of her tray managed to make its way into my still damp hair and (uniquely) ironed top. Even Slug was soon sporting several spoonfuls, which she did her best to lick greedily off her shaggy coat.

Not having time to change, I brushed out my hair and wiped my top clean as best I could with a damp cloth. Despite the promising-looking September morning, I hoped it would be cold enough to leave my jacket on to hide the stains. I finally left just after seven, with both Molly and Slug sulking in the kitchen, while Donal resigned himself to what was going to be a troublesome day off.

It was after half-eight by the time I arrived at my destination. I pulled into the long, railed driveway, and admired the array of mares and foals grazing lazily in the last rays of the summer sun.

I was almost feeling optimistic until I got to the delegates' parking lot and wedged my grubby Opel Corsa in between a brand new BMW on one side and an equally gleaming Land Cruiser on the other. The whole parking area was taken up with similar vehicles, one or two of which were sign-written with logos of exclusive equine hospitals.

The reception itself was intimidating to an impostor like myself, with rows and rows of framed photographs of winning horses hung along the lengthy entrance hall, many of which were bred by the owners of the hotel.

It didn't help when I arrived into the foyer to find that the expensively clad delegates were almost exclusively male. I quickly detoured to the toilets to give myself time to mentally regroup. Reappearing back out, I slid in behind a coffee table and busied myself pouring a coffee, frantically trying to look like part of the group.

'Excuse me!' a cry came towards me from one of the suits.

Maybe they're not as bad as I'm making them out to be, I thought to myself, making my way over to join the group at the table.

'Excuse me,' he continued, 'four coffees over here and more milk.'

'What?' I replied, stupidly.

'Four coffees, please. And another jug of milk,' he repeated and he looked away before I could reply.

Fuming, I picked up one of the sets of lecture notes and made my way into the conference hall where the lectures were to be held. The scattering of colleagues ignored me as I tried to pick out a friendly eye. Eventually, I sat down in the middle of a row and waited as the others filed in. The meeting was well attended and by nine o' clock every seat in the house was full – apart from one on either side of me and a couple in the front row.

Although I knew that equine veterinary practice was at that time primarily a male-dominated area, I was still surprised to see that of the twenty-four delegates, only three were female. One, not much older than me, I later discovered had been sent to take notes for her boss. The other was a hardened-looking horsey type who seemed to be well in with the rest of the delegates.

The usual format for such meetings, that would carry on over a number of days, was that everyone would have to introduce themselves to the group. However, in this case,

Jason, the lecturer, having introduced himself and his seemingly endless lifetime achievements, simply glanced quickly up and down the lines, as everyone seemed to know everyone else already. When he came to one of the other women, he didn't give her a chance to say a word. 'Emma,' he informed the crowd, 'has the privilege of having joined ranks with Mike O'Dee and she's here to take notes', and he continued on, obviously not deeming her worthy of any further attention. I later discover that her name was, in fact, Lucy, and that she had qualified four years previously and, having spent several stud seasons in both hemispheres of the world, had then gone on to do a master's in equine reproduction. When he came to me, Jason peered at his notes before looking up to ask, 'And who are you here for?'

I introduced myself and the name of the practice I worked for.

'Riverside Veterinary Clinic. Mixed practice is it?' he asked disdainfully. 'A few calls to the local piebald, is it? I suppose they'd look the same as a Friesian cow!'

A great guffaw of laughter broke out among the ranks before he passed on to the next row.

The topic for the morning was respiratory disease, so I tried to concentrate on the lecture and ignore my sense of alienation. The basic anatomy was followed by physiology, with nothing new to add. Then the eminent equine specialist moved on to his pet topic of video endoscopy. Video endoscopy consists of putting a horse on a treadmill, not unlike what you would see in your local gym and passing an endoscope, with a tiny camera, up the nostril of the horse and then down to various levels of the airways. With the endoscope in place, the horse is then put through its paces while a picture of the airway is displayed on a screen. For the first twenty or so slides of some horse's larynx, I was engrossed. Then my mind began to wander. What, I wondered, would Larry Byrne's mare's larynx look like – the one who had a history of grinding to a halt a half mile or so into strenuous exercise? Or better still, Pauline Thomson's half-breed, who could jump anything put in front of her, but made a most peculiar noise while doing so. And then I realised that I would never know, as, to the best of my knowledge, at the time there wasn't a single video endoscope facility in the entire country. As far as I knew, all the vets attending the course were Irish and yet they were all nodding knowingly at the slide show. It was starting to bug me, so that by the time the lecture came to an end, and questions were invited, I tentatively raised my hand.

Jason didn't look too pleased to see my hand and he took every other question in the room before he came to me.

'Sorry,' I enquired, 'but where is the nearest endoscope facility?'

'Oh, don't be bothering your head about it, dear,' he replied blithely. 'A stethoscope is the only sort of a scope you'll ever get to use with your piebalds.'

Although amidst the laughter that followed, one or two of the delegates did throw me a sympathetic glance, I noticed that no one mentioned where the nearest facility was.

With the questions and answers over, a tea-break was announced. We all made our way down the carpeted stairway to a cosy lounge where three tables were placed around an open fire, each set for eight people.

At least, I though to myself, it would be some consolation to have a decent bit of food without singing nursery rhymes or having it slopped all over me. The homemade scones and Danish pastries justified themselves along with the steaming pots of tea and coffee that were laid out at the top of the room. In turn, we all filled a cup and loaded a plate from the woven baskets. The first few delegates sat down around the table nearest to the fire, filling the eight seats at that table. As I was ninth in line, I took the first seat at the next table and busied myself buttering a scone while wondering who I would be seated beside. I didn't have long to wait as I saw the person after me turn towards my table and then, stopping in his tracks, turn away to go to a third table. I watched in silence as each vet that followed joined the previous one at that table, ignoring me where I sat alone. Finally, thankfully, Lucy, alias Emma, came over and smiled gratefully as she sat down beside me.

'Friendly lot, aren't they?' I offered, after we had introduced ourselves.

'You said it,' she replied. 'You should try working with them.'

Clearly, despite Lucy's addition, we were no more attractive and the remaining delegates pulled the chairs from our table and squeezed them in around the others. It was certainly a closed club.

If I hadn't been so stunned, I might almost have laughed at their ignorance as their loud, brash voices recounted their tales of wonder in the veterinary world, each more interested in their own story than anybody else's. At any other courses that I had attended, the breaks usually found most people talking about the cases that had gone wrong and trying to pick up tips from others, so that a break almost became like a professional confessional, with mutual commiserations and sometimes advice to follow. It seemed, however, that in the equine world, there were no such misfortunes or bad days.

It wasn't until the talk at the next table came around to the poor fertility rates that seemed to be plaguing horse breeders since the previous season that Lucy began to prick up her ears. Having spent two of her four seasons in New Zealand working exclusively in equine fertility, she obviously had an interest in and considerable knowledge of the topic. Although each member of the table outlined the success of their techniques, none could deny that it had been a poor season, with many of the top yards performing badly.

Although it was difficult to drown out the heated debates at the other tables, Lucy began to talk with increasing enthusiasm about her experience during her stud seasons as home and abroad. It turned out that the mini lecture in equine reproduction she gave me over all the breaks through the day became the most useful and practical thing I learnt during the entire course.

The second module the following month was purely surgical and, with no surgical faculties to speak of, nor the likelihood of there ever being any in Riverside, it was unlikely that I would get to use any of the knowledge so begrudgingly offered during the day. The third module confined itself to dermatology, never a rewarding subject as skin cases are notoriously difficult to treat. I was frustrated on the long drive home, realising that I hadn't learnt anything useful that I could put into practice and change what I had been doing up until now. The fourth and fifth modules were to be run as a two-day event over a weekend. On the Friday evening, when I arrived home from work, Molly greeted me with a thin, drawn-out wail, a high temperature and an unusual-looking rash, which, in Crumlin hospital in the early hours of the morning, was eventually declared to be an undiagnosed virus.

On the Sunday morning as were being discharged, thankfully with Molly back in full spirits, although I myself was still shattered, I vaguely wondered how the talk on foal medicine was going and ironically wondered if any one had missed me. It turned out that I need not have worried, as Lucy and myself kept in touch, and from then on I ended up ringing her for advice, which was always freely given, when presented with any unusual horse case.

I wasn't surprised when, two years later, she left the hallowed ground of Mike O'Dee and set up her own highly successful practice, specialising solely in equine reproduction.

CHAPTER SIX

THE BALD EAGLE

I feel that birds get a rough deal when it comes to equality. I do remember going to one avian lecture in college given by some expert who ran a referral clinic solely dedicated to birds. I think they had to import him from somewhere in England, as there was no one available locally to do the lecture. I'm sure we must have had other lectures on avian medicine, though doubtfully in avian surgery, but, either way, whatever gems of wisdom were imparted to us in college, certainly they hadn't left much of an impression on me.

One of my earlier locum jobs, in a mixed practice run by a larger-than-life character called Joe, typified the attitude of veterinary interest in birds. One quiet afternoon, while I was sitting in the office signing TB cards, a pleasant look-ing young lady arrived in. She was, she informed the receptionist, newly moved into the area and had three 'rare and expensive parrots', as she described them. Was the vet familiar with birds, she enquired? Sarah, the middle-aged mother of five children, who had worked in the practice since before they were all born, dismissed the flimsy-looking creature before her as she replied in her droll monotone, 'Oh he's familiar with birds, all right – but not the feathered ones!'

In one of the first clinics where I saw practice as a student, the four vets were discussing their early days after graduation and laughing at how they had handled their first consultations.

'Mine,' said the oldest, 'was a bird. Can you imagine it? I might have managed to vaccinate a puppy, but there was this bird sitting in its cage with blood bubbling out of its beak.'

'What did you do?' laughed another. 'Take him in for a head X-ray?'

'I told the owner that he probably fell off his perch and bumped his beak. I tried to pack it with some cotton wool, but the thing bit me and there was so much blood you couldn't see who it was coming from. Worst thing was, as she was going out the door, I was trying to salvage myself and I told her not to worry, that nose bleeds were very common in canaries. Well, I nearly died when she told me it was a budgie!'

Luckily, when I myself qualified and began to work, I managed to escape the feathered patients for quite some time, but at Riverside Clinic one day, my luck ran out. On one of my first evening clinics, I opened the waiting-room door to see a spacious cage containing the dreaded avian. Other than knowing for sure that it was a budgie, I was stumped. The fact that the luckless creature was suffering from diarrhoea was clearly evident from the foul-smelling tail feathers. The owner had already rung the other neighbouring practice who claimed not to treat 'exotics'. I had no option but to extrapolate from my knowledge of other species and treat the bird with an anti-parasite medication and the only antibiotic that I knew was licensed for birds. Luckily, the antibiotics came with an idiot-proof dosing guide for exotics, presumably designed for the client, but which, I suspected, many vets kept handy in their bottom drawers.

After issuing a grave prognosis, I didn't expect to see the budgie again. I was delighted, initially, when the owner rang to say that Peter was doing well, and by the weekend he had made a miraculous recovery. Although the usefulness of my intervention was dubious, Peter's owner was nonetheless very enthusiastic. The unfortunate result of this was that my reputation as a bird vet grew. From then on, a regular trickle of birds began to make their way into the surgery and despite the fact that my limited knowledge led only to limited success, Peter's owner was obviously an important figure in the local bird world and my followers remained undeterred.

As my reputation looked set to last, I invested in some heavy-duty avian manuals, hoping they might enlighten me. Along with the trickle of cases, my research allowed me to add some credibility to my reputation.

Just as I was beginning to enjoy my status as bird vet (much to the amusement and relief of both Seamus and Arthur), things began to get out of hand. I wasn't overly worried when Sean, the local forester, arrived in one day.

We knew him well, as he kept his own horse and had a few working spaniels. But, apart from his own animals, he also had a great interest in wildlife and, in particular, birds. He was the nicest type of client: terribly knowledgeable but always open to advice. In all honesty, I'd say that I learnt as much from him as he did from me in the time we knew each other.

He was the type of person who was always in good form, but today his face was grim. The forest he managed had attracted a pair of nesting buzzards, which he watched with the care of a proud parent.

'Wait till you see this,' he said glumly as he hauled out a huge bird-bag, usually used for transporting swans. I was stunned to see not the graceful head of a swan, but that of a buzzard, flopping out of the bag.

'Wow! It is a buzzard, isn't it?' I asked, unused to seeing one up close.

'One of the pair nesting in the forest,' he confirmed. 'I heard the other one shrieking while I was down with the saplings and I thought maybe something was attacking the nest. I found this one collapsed below it.'

Between us, we examined the bird. Initially, I was enthralled to have access to such a beautiful creature at such close quarters. The wing span, at full stretch, was wider than the length of our generously-sized consulting table. The mottled brown breast was well-rounded, indicating that the bird had been healthy until whatever catastrophe had struck.

A detailed examination, with Sean keeping a firm hold of the powerful talons, didn't reveal much, other than that the bird was severely weakened. I scanned through various forms of infectious diseases, poisonings, trauma, among other things, but I wasn't convinced by any of my tentative diagnoses. Being the Friday evening of a bank holiday weekend, no other help was available.

'All we can do,' I said to Sean, 'is treat the symptoms and see how he gets on.'

Adjusting the little bit of knowledge I did have, I gave him fluids infused with a carefully measured amount of glucose, some antibiotic and a steroid to combat his shocked state. Sean took the bird home with him, but the next day, although the buzzard seemed to be a bit stronger, he was still unable to rise. By the Sunday morning, I was becoming more concerned as there was no further improvement and his weight was dropping despite force-feeding him select cuts of natural prey. 'Why don't we radiograph him?' I suggested. 'It might just give us some clues.'

'Whatever you think,' replied Sean. 'Sure, it can do no harm anyway.'

Although the buzzard was still very weak, the powerful beak and talons still worried me. Extrapolating from a sedation regime that I had used on other birds, I cautiously injected a lowered dose into the patient. Then I pulled out the largest cassette that we had in the practice, with the appropritate film. But the usual bags that we used to position the patient worried me due to their weight, which I felt might inhibit the bird's delicate breathing. Ingeniously, I thought, I used some Sellotape to tape his neck in place as this plan had worked well with the few reptiles I'd previously needed to radiograph. Despite our efforts, the resultant radiograph, although spectacular, shed no further light on the mystery. Problems arose when the buzzard came around a bit quicker than expected, probably as a result of my overly-cautious anaesthetic dose. The Sellotape was by now firmly stuck to the bird's feathers and in my haste to free him, the feathers came out with the tape, leaving a two-centimetre bald collar in the previously immaculate plumage.

'He looks more like a bald eagle now,' joked Sean.

I had mixed feelings on the Tuesday morning when I rang the Department of Agriculture to report the bird, as it is illegal to keep any bird of prey without a special permit. I wasn't sure exactly who in the Department was responsible and I was put on hold a few times, and passed from one office to another. I was eventually put on to a severe-sounding woman who told me that the office in question could not be contacted at present and she was dealing with the enquiries.

I briefly explained the situation.

'Well, if you have the appropriate licence for keeping a bird in captivity there should be no problem,' she rapped back.

'That's exactly why I'm ringing you,' I continued, patiently. 'The bird was brought in over the weekend, after your offices were closed. I'm trying to find out how I can get a licence now or who I can pass the bird on to.'

'Well, the Department rules clearly state that you need to have a permit to keep a bird of prey.'

'Yes, I am aware of that,' I explained, feeling slightly less patient. 'That's exactly why I'm ringing you.'

'But that's no good now. You have to get the permit before you get the bird,' she continued in her official voice. 'You could end up in deep water over this one,' she advised me gravely.

'Excuse me,' I carried on, becoming increasingly exacerbated, 'what was I supposed to do? Leave the bird in the forest for the long weekend and hope it wouldn't die in the time it would take you to process the licence?'

'Well, all I know is that the regulations state that –'

'I know what the regulations state,' I snapped. 'Now, would you mind telling me how I can go about getting the appropriate licence?'

'All I know,' she repeated, 'is that you can't keep a bird of prey without a licence.'

'Right! Fine so! I'll dump it back out in the forest and let it die. At least that way we'll all be happy that we haven't breached any Department regulations,' and I slammed down the phone.

'Relax the head,' laughed Sean, as I fumed at the stupidity of it all. 'Sure, what are they going to do? Come out and take it off you? They would be scared of their lives of a buzzard. Tell her to come and take it if she wants it,' and we both burst out laughing at the image of her arriving out in an office suit and high heels to seize the patient!

That evening, I sent an e-mail to the Department of Agriculture informing them that we were treating a bird of prey and inviting them to take charge of it. We're still waiting ...

Meanwhile, the buzzard, while gaining strength, was still semi-paralysed and showed no inclination to eat without us force-feeding him. He clearly wasn't impressed with our intervention, but we managed to stomach-tube him twice daily and over the next few days his weight levelled out. By the end of the week, he was able to lift himself up and I gladly left it to Sean to handle the powerful bird while I administered to it! On the following Sunday, he took his first mouse, gobbling it greedily, and on the Monday morning, Sean almost didn't make it out of the pen after feeding him. The great bird stretched his wings to full span and, shrieking angrily, flew at the door just as Sean bolted it from the outside. For another two days we threw in his food, injected with his medication, and finally it was time to release him.

We met early on the Wednesday morning, and with a lot more skill than I would ever have, Sean managed to capture the bird while I ran in with the bag. Once he was firmly secured, we bundled him into the back of the van and drove to the woods. The dawn was just breaking on this magical morning and we were almost deafened by the volume of the dawn chorus as we unloaded our patient. He struggled violently as we carried him to the edge of the forest where he had been found. Quickly, Sean untied the strings and just as we were about to undo the final body string, a shrill shriek sounded out from above us. Through the dim light we saw the mate high up in the trees as she continued to scream in anger at us. By now, our patient was replying in full voice as his efforts to escape became more determined. Suddenly the mate began to swoop down towards us and with one look at the vast stature of the rapidly approaching wings, we abandoned our charge in unison and ran to the van.

'Do you think they would attack?' I asked Sean when we were safely inside.

'I don't know,' he replied, 'but I sure as hell wasn't hanging around to find out. Ah sure, we'll get yer one in the Department down to inspect them and find out,' and he broke out into a great roar of laughter.

Meanwhile the pair were reunited and within a few seconds the buzzard had freed himself of the bag and the two rose high up above the forest before starting to circle, shrieking and screaming with what we, maybe romantically, ascribed to joy at being reunited.

From then on, Sean kept me regularly updated as he often spotted the pair in the forest. Our bird was easily recognisable as the only buzzard with a large bald patch around the base of his neck! Despite my well-intentioned blunderings, the 'bald eagle' had survived.

CHAPTER SEVEN

PYJAMA PARTY

I f I had known what sort of a day it was going to be when the phone shrilled in my ear just before six in the morning, I probably wouldn't have picked it up. In my stupefied state of semi-slumber, I reached over and grunted sleepily into the receiver. Seamus, the boss, always answered the calls at night himself and then passed them on to either myself or Arthur, depending on who was on duty. At least it meant that I didn't have to bother pretending to be full of the joys of spring when I answered. At times, it amazed me how we communicated a comprehensible message with a series of grunts and monosyllables. It was no different this time.

'Cow with a prolapse. Peter Jones. Ballinahinch. On the Wexford road just after The Coachman pub.'

'Okay so. I'll go on out.'

I dropped the receiver without waiting for a reply, knowing that if I did, all I would hear would be the dead tone.

I lay back and closed my eyes for just a couple of

moments before hauling myself out and falling into my clothes. There is an art with night calls which, with practice, allows you to time accurately the moment at which you come out of automatic-pilot mode and actually wake up. When perfected, it allows you to dress and drive to the call while still feeling like you are in bed. It was probably because of this that it didn't dawn on me immediately that Ballinahinch was well beyond the usual practice boundaries. It was going to take me over an hour to get there, at which stage I was going to be met by an irate farmer – Seamus had an unfortunate habit of telling the farmer to expect me in twenty minutes. Local geographics never seemed to offer any excuse.

Slug eyed me balefully as I picked up the car keys and with a martyred look she slumped down the stairs and out to the car. When I opened the car door for her, instead of jumping in as she usually would, she just stood there. Obviously she was good at automatic-pilot mode too. I picked her up and deposited her on the passenger seat where she curled into a ball and never stirred for the rest of the journey.

I'd got about five miles down the road when the phone rang again. I quickly calculated that if the call was from Seamus to say that the cow had calved, I could probably make it back to bed for another twenty minutes at least.

'Yeah,' I answered.

'Are you there yet?'

'No. My private helicopter's out of order this morning.'

My sarcasm was lost as Seamus continued, 'James Manus. Ewe lambing – says he'll meet you in the surgery in half an hour.'

'How the hell will I get there in half an hour?' I yelled down the line. 'I'm still on my way to the prolapse in Balli-nahinch.'

The line went dead.

I mentally tried to calm myself in case the anger would interrupt my semi-conscious state.

Before I knew it, I had travelled the long road all the way past the practice and some twenty miles further. When I finally reached The Coachman pub I had abso-lutely no recollection of how I had got there. Almost immediately after it, I was flashed down by two men and a young boy. I hadn't even opened the door before the abuse hit me.

'What sort of a bloody service is this? We've been wait-ing here nearly an hour for you. We put the call through before six. I suppose you thought you'd have a bit of breakfast as you weren't in a rush. Well, I can tell you, we haven't had our bloody breakfast yet.'

I was stunned by the ferocity of the attack. Normally I found the farmers very easy going and I was used to retali-ating to the good-natured slagging matches that often took place. The bit about the breakfast really got to me as the rumbling in my stomach was giving me some forceful reminders of my hunger.

I stared coldly at what I assumed to be father and son, one a miniature version of the other. Beside them, the stockman stood, staring accusingly at me, arms folded, waiting to attack my reply. I raised myself to my full height and replied in a quiet, controlled voice. 'I came immediately on getting the call. Your yard is well beyond the outskirts of the practice. Maybe you should think of using a vet closer to you.'

'Don't you get smart with me!' the father replied furiously. 'There's no time to be getting other vets now.'

'Well, maybe you should have thought of that first. Now if you could show me the cow, please? Unfortunately I don't have time to stand around arguing. I have more calls to get to before I get my breakfast.'

The usual reason for a client to use a practice far away was because they had been refused service from the local vets for non-payment or other reasons. In this case, I could clearly see why the local vets probably refused to deal with these particular clients, payment or not.

The father's face reddened in fury as he stomped off into the shed with the son indignantly marching behind. As I followed him, a knot of frustration settled in my stomach. An unpleasant job could be made so much worse if the farmer was unhelpful. I counted the minutes until I would be out of the yard and on the road to the next call, although my farmer with the ewe lambing would probably be equally furious by the time I got back to the surgery.

My mood darkened when I saw my patient: a large, highly strung, Charolais cow, running loose with a bunch of her equally neurotic comrades. As she bucked and wheeled with the rest of them, her massively engorged prolapsed uterus was clearly visible as it bobbed up and down behind her.

The father sneered at me from the far side of the shed. 'Well now, what do you make of that one? Now we'll see if female vets are all they're cracked up to be.'

'Yeah, now we'll see,' echoed his miniature.

I glared coldly at him. I was well used to the typical 'female vet' slagging and normally joined in the crack, but whatever about hearing it from the openly aggressive father, I was not going to take it from his half-pint son.

As I watched my patient's upturned heels disappearing at speed past me, I raised my eyes to heaven and asked the father if it had occurred to him to have a pen prepared to separate her out for the job.

'You did have a whole hour to get ready,' I reminded him sweetly.

I quickly assessed how and where we would enclose her in the shed and became increasingly irritated by the reluctance of any of them to do anything but moan at each request I made. I had become used to the helpful farmers in our area who would go out of their way to assist you, and was normally amused by the constant reminders of 'Mind yourself now that you don't get hurt', or 'Stand back there and I'll do that for you.' At times it frustrated me, but right now any sign of helpfulness wouldn't have gone astray.

With the cow finally penned in a corner, I hung precariously over the gate with a freshly made rope halter in an attempt to drop it over the angrily swishing head. Three sets of resentful eyes bored into my back, willing me to fail. I almost felt their intense disappointment when it dropped neatly over her head at the first attempt and I was able to tie her securely to the only beam in the shed that would have any hope of restraining the tonne of fuming flesh.

I carefully drew up a calculated extra-strong dose of sedative, knowing full well that the usual dose would be like throwing saline into the angry Charolais. As I waited for the medication to take effect, the phone rang. I could have cried when I saw Seamus's number on the screen, wondering what other calls he might have lined up for me. 'I'm here in Jones's. I'm going to be a while,' I replied, in a neutral tone, indicating that the farmers were standing beside me listening to every word I said.

'Oh lovely,' he replied cheerfully, obviously the better for his leisurely breakfast. 'Those cattle are absolutely stark raving mad. And, by the way, did I forget to tell you that those Joneses are a dangerous crew? They ended up taking one the vets from Edwardstown Veterinary Clinic to court over a calving – that's why we have the pleasure of their business now. But, sure, you've probably worked that one out by now. Anyway, I'm in the factory for the morning so I'm absolutely no use to you, but sure if you're still at it by midday, I'll come out to give you a hand. Have a nice day now.'

His loud, booming laugh was cut short as he hung up while I fought desperately to retain my self-control in front of the inquisitive farmers.

'Was that the boss man, then?' asked the father.

'I suppose he has to come out to help you,' added the son, arms folded, leaning haughtily up against the farm gate.

'Seamus is in the factory today. Why would he be coming out here?' I asked, wondering if they always expected two vets to do one job.

'Sure, you're fresh to the job,' said the father. 'You probably haven't ever done one of these before.'

'Yeah and sure you're only a woman,' added the half-pint, while the stockman grinned silently to himself in the corner.

As I made my way out to the car to gather the equipment, my feeling of doom deepened. By the time I had positioned the cow and was started on the laborious task of carefully cleaning the fragile organ, the stockman had disappeared, obviously bored by the novelty of a female vet. I was reduced to a duet of continuous snide comments with son repeating father, answered by father's uproarious laughter each time. Obviously the training process to produce such a creature was intensive.

Replacing a prolapse is always slow and tedious, but in this case, compounded by the hostile environment, it seemed to drag on.

'You're obviously not in a rush, are you?' began the father.

'She's not in a rush, Dad, is she?'

My temper was beginning to fray. At the last assault, I stood up and made my way over to where the son stood, casually leaning over a bale of straw. He jumped in fright at my sudden speed.

'Now listen here, you,' I began, breathing deeply to retain the calm, controlled voice. 'Sooner or later you're going to get the stuffing knocked out of you and you'll probably be a nicer child for it, but if you don't get out of here quickly, it's going to be sooner rather than later'.

He took one look at his father, who stood gaping as though wounded, and turned and ran out the shed door.

I didn't see him again.

'That's no way to speak to a young chap,' began the father, in a new-found subdued tone.

'If he can't take it, he shouldn't give it and if you don't like it, you should get another vet. Now, do you want the job done or don't you?'

'Well, you'd better finish your own mess,' he replied lamely.

The adrenaline rush gave me new strength and within minutes the prolapse was back in place. In peaceful silence I placed the strong vaginal sutures. After the sudden exertion I stood up, delighted with my improved status, feeling that I wouldn't have to take any more verbal abuse from this man. He stood silently, staring at me with a mixture of respect and bewilderment painted across his face. The sweat dripped off me as I pulled off my water-proofs to go into the dairy to wash. I was feeling so smug that I didn't notice his face lose the look of almost admira-tion and crumple into helpless laughter. As I splashed the cold water over myself I caught sight of what I thought was my shirt sleeves rolled up my arms. It was then that it struck me that in my hurry to get dressed that morning, I had forgotten to take off my pyjamas. Little red and blue bears bounced up and down across the furry material.

I tried to ignore the endless mirth as I hurriedly scrawled out a bill and took my shattered dignity with me back into the car. The dirt thrown up from my skid marks hid the sight of the farmer, doubled up in laughter, as I drove furi-ously out of the yard and towards the surgery for my next flurry of abuse.

CHAPTER EIGHT

SPECIAL INDULGENCES

'**G**o on in,' urged the oldest of the three lads, giving a good dig in the ribs to the one who was holding the dog. There was a bit of muttering and shuffling going on between the three of them before the middle one grabbed the dog and came towards me while the other two turned to sit in the waiting room.

I noticed the oldest of the three cast an experienced eye over the shelves of expensive horse and cattle wormers at Riverside Clinic.

'Right, lads. All of you in here together,' I called to them.

'No. Go on, Jock. You go in,' gestured the oldest, sullenly avoiding my eye.

'Lads,' I said firmly, 'either wait outside in the car park or come in here.'

When I clearly heard the word 'bitch' in the mutterings

that followed, I was quite sure they weren't referring to any canine.

In fact, the dog seemed to be the only enthusiastic member of the group. He swished his tail languidly as he approached me, his seemingly never-ending tongue hanging out as he raised a paw to me in greeting.

'What's the problem, so?' I began, bending down to sink my hands in the long, glossy coat of the dog, noticing the expensive studded collar with the incongruous blue rope.

'We want ye to put 'im down. Give 'im a needle or somethin'.'

I looked up in alarm at the three faces that were studiously avoiding mine. 'You what?'

'Me ma said to have 'im put asleep,' responded the young one eventually, without raising his eyes to mine.

My mind was in turmoil as I tried to assess the situation.

Unfortunately, it was all too common for either the parents or the children to become bored with even as handsome a pet as this one and demand the animal be euthanised; occasionally with the added 'unless you can find someone for him yourself.' And yet something didn't add up. This was no ordinary pet that had gradually become neglected as a result of an owner's waning interest. To buy myself time, I began to examine him and I couldn't help but notice the sleek, glossy coat that could only have resulted from a good, balanced diet and hours of regular grooming. The nails were short, well worn from long, regular walks and as he sank his enormous head in my lap, I knew that this was a dog that was very much cherished and cared for.

The lads shuffled around restlessly as I carried out my examination, offering no clues.

'Why?' I asked, addressing the oldest. 'Why does she want him put down?'

'Dunno,' he shrugged, avoiding my eye. 'Just does.'

'Why?' I said to the next one. He stared uncomfortably at the floor before the third one blurted out, 'He bit me brudder,' gesturing at the one holding the lead. All three nodded in unison, suddenly enthusiastic.

Although biting a child is totally unforgivable, looking at this gentle giant, I just didn't believe it as he stared at me with placid, trusting eyes; had he licked him to death, it might have been a different matter.

'Well,' I said finally, 'you'll have to get one of your parents down with you. I'll need them to sign a consent form.'

I might as well have dropped a bomb, and I knew by the disgusted expressions that my gut instinct was right.

'But I'm eighteen,' assured the biggest one, looking up for the first time but still avoiding my eye.

'Sorry,' I lied smoothly, 'but you have to be twenty-one.'

'I'm twenty one,' squeaked the smallest of the three, but he was rapidly deflated as the other two turned on him: 'Shut up, ye bleedin' eejit, ye.'

'Shut up yerselves, will ye,' he replied, turning puce.

'Listen, lads, I don't have time for this. Go off and get one of your parents and come back after lunch,' I told them, fairly sure it would be the last I would see of the trio. 'No way!' I said as they made to go and pick up the rope. 'I'll hang on to him until you get back.'

'But he's my bleedin' dog,' retorted the little lad.

'Lads. Out! Now!' I said firmly, holding the door open for them.

They took one look at me and realising that I was serious, they barrelled out the door amidst much elbowing and curses.

'Ye'r a mad fecking bitch, ye are,' roared the last over his shoulder as they raced up the street.

'So, what's your story, big fella?' I asked the dog, gently stroking his silky ears as he gazed up trustingly at me.

Quickly, I set up a kennel for him and having made sure that he had a comfortable bed and a dish of fresh water, I went off for a delayed lunch, resolving to start ringing around the local pounds and shelters before going out on my afternoon calls to see if he had been reported missing.

I hardly managed to swallow my sandwich in the local deli as two people caught me, before I had even sat down, to 'ask just a quick question' which took up most of the remaining precious minutes.

At two minutes to two, I was hurriedly unlocking the surgery door when I noticed a middle-aged man in clerical garb rushing towards me.

'Excuse me,' he began, out of breath, 'could I possibly have a minute of your time, please?'

Here we go again, I thought to myself wearily, knowing that now I wouldn't have a chance to trace the dog until that evening.

'My dog has gone missing, you see,' he told me as I nodded my consent with what I hoped was a pleasant smile.

My heart missed a beat, and I heard myself ask casually,

'What type of dog is he?'

'Oh the most beautiful dog, you just couldn't miss him. He's a big long-haired German Shepherd.'

'Right, well, if you'd just like to step inside and take a seat, I'll be with you in a moment,' I said as calmly as I could, not wanting to raise the man's hopes. I quickly let myself out the back door to the kennel area.

'Come on, big fella,' I called to the dog, who was looking a little bit agitated by the confinement.

I led him out to the waiting area and as soon as his head came around the door the priest leapt up ecstatically. 'Oh, thank God you've found him. Prince, where have you been?' he cried as he fell to his knees and wrapped himself around the giant shaggy neck. Prince, as I now knew him, whimpered and cried in answer, obviously as delighted as his master by the reunion.

When the pair had sufficiently composed themselves, I filled in Fr Jim Hanley on the story.

'Well, the little ...!' He trailed off without finishing what I assume would have been a most unpriestly sentence.

As I described the lads, he nodded wearily. 'I know them, all right. Jock, Dermo and JP. They've been hassling me for months. Prince is the only reason they haven't been able to do much damage but, God bless him, he's such a trusting soul he'd go with anyone. When I think of what could have happened if you hadn't noticed ...' and he shuddered at the thought.

'They're not bad lads, really,' he continued. 'Usual story – the parents aren't up to much and they've just run wild, but by God I wouldn't have let them away with this,' he said fiercely, hugging the delighted Prince as his eyes filled with tears.

And I felt for this man; this man who had obviously sacrificed his life for his beliefs in an effort to do good for people who clearly didn't want it.

'How can I ever thank you?' he said, gripping my hand. 'If there is ever a thing in the world I can do for you, won't you please let me know?' he beseeched me.

'Ah Father, think nothing of it,' I assured him, only too delighted to have reunited the dog with his rightful owner. 'Sure, maybe you could give me a few indulgences,' I laughed.

'I'll give you a life's supply of them, for sure,' he answered as the happy pair left the surgery.

CHAPTER NINE

TWIN LAMBS

I t wasn't the first time I had been up to McFadden's and the call this afternoon suited me just perfectly. It had been a busy morning, testing cattle in an inadequate yard with a rare type of unsociable farmer and I was in need of a bit of genuine hospitality and goodwill to restore my faith in the clients.

Even driving along the winding road up through the hills did much to cheer my spirit. Tom and Mary Mc Fadden were born into farming and despite the ongoing modernisation all around them, the yard itself had changed little since they had first taken it over. Although they now bought in hay from local contractors, the only tractor that ever ripped across the small but well-maintained fields would be one of a neighbour. George, the donkey, was solely responsible for manure removal and spreading, for loading hay and drawing grain, and the hundred and one other tasks that were always to be done around the admittedly small and uneconomic farm.

When I first met the couple, I was enchanted by Tom, with his well-weathered face and twinkling eyes, and by Mary, with her inherent strength that came from a life of physical toil. Nonetheless, I was concerned about introducing myself into a farm where time had stood still. I wondered how they would accept the modern medicines and methods that had become routine in the life of a vet. But my worry was needless. On my first visit, I had been called out to dehorn cattle, a task which, despite my usual misgivings, went relatively well. As I pulled out the embryotomy wire to saw off the immature horns, Mary, especially, was fascinated.

'Well, I never,' she declared, 'it's just like the old-fashioned cheese cutter my mother used to use.'

The description stuck and every time I appeared, I would hear the familiar cry of 'Tom, come on out. It's the vet with the cheese cutter!' followed by much mirth and merriment all around.

Despite their acceptance of modernisation, Tom and Mary had chosen not to invest in new ways, knowing that their meagre small-holding would not support much expensive investment. However, after my first few visits, I came to admire the rude good health of their collection of suckler cows, horned sheep, the single sow and the bewildering array of fowl that always seemed to be underfoot. The lack of pressure of the modern yard allowed them the luxury of attention to detail and the priceless tender loving care which seemed to have been lost in bigger more 'efficient' holdings.

My patient today was a large, horned ewe, known to the

department as IE 42-509121 610, which I noted down for the clinical records, but, to Tom and Mary, she was known quite simply as Edel ('She was the fifth lamb out of Patricia – always just a single ewe lamb she had,' confided Mary, making me wonder yet again about the convoluted traceability schemes dreamed up by those in the know).

Edel, like her mother before her, I was told, had carried on the tradition of always having a single ewe lamb. This was her first time to require veterinary attention and as I inserted a carefully lubricated hand into her vagina, I realised why. Although she was a big ewe for her breed, the pair of cloven hooves that lay, side by side in the vaginal passage, seemed more suited to a large, roomy Texel. I was just about able to get my hand far back enough to feel the tip of the nose, all perfectly aligned and in normal presentation, but I knew without a doubt that there was no way this lamb would be delivered in the normal fashion. Tom and Mary waited anxiously as I squeezed hard between the digits of the hoof to ascertain if the lamb was still alive. Eventually, I felt the reflex jerk, as the leg pulled back assuring me that, at least for the moment, all was well with the lamb.

A caesarean is a relatively expensive option, especially on a small hill farm, but I had a good feeling, even before I discussed the options, that Edel's guardians would want to give it a go.

In a few minutes, the operation table was prepared and Edel lay, carefully restrained by Tom's huge and capable hands, on a bed of golden straw. Having prepared the surgical site, I injected local anaesthetic into the skin and underlying muscle, where I would make my incision. We chatted for a few minutes as I continued to scrub the site while waiting for the area to be numbed. Once I was happy that Edel had no feeling, I incised the taut skin, stained brown from the disinfectant with which I had carefully scrubbed her flank. The combined smells of the surgical spirit and the clear, fresh air around us made the place smell as clean as any sterile theatre. Once through the muscle layers, it wasn't difficult to locate the glistening uterus as it seemed to take up the entire abdomen. Within minutes, I had located the joint of the hind leg of the lamb, but I had to extend my usual incision within the uterus to allow for the enormous, well-filled rump of the lamb to pull through. Apart from being covered in placental fluid, with the give-away floppy ears still clinging to the head, the lamb was so big he could have been mistaken for a two-month-old. By the time I had finished stitching the rapidly contracting uterus, he was up on his feet and butting hard at his mother who encouraged him with a deep-throated voice, accepting all.

'Well, that's a first for the family,' said Tom, gently tossing the heavyweight upside-down. 'That's the first ram lamb in that line for two generations.'

'But still only the single as always,' added Mary.

Reluctantly declining the offer of a cup of tea, I was soon scrubbed and packed. As I drove away, I was delighted to see mother and lamb settling down for a good feed, although Gulliver (promptly named after the giant in *Gulliver's Travels*) almost had to stoop to reach his mother's udder.

Although prior to Gulliver's dramatic entrance I hadn't visited the Mc Fadden's in many months, as usual, bad luck comes in threes. It was only two weeks before I was to return, this time to a collapsed suckler. The long, winding road held no charm for me today as, in the race against time, it seemed to get longer with each twist and bend. The history of the cow worried me. 'She's a scrawny little one,' Tom had told me over the phone. 'She had her calf there a while back and hasn't picked up too well since. I thought she was a bit stiff in herself yesterday, but she seemed agitated when I tried to have a look at her. I found her down this morning, over beyond the gorse bushes. I don't know if I'll manage it, but if ye like I can go up with the dog and try and get her up and into the shed for you,' he added eagerly.

'Thanks, Tom, but no. Not this time,' I assured him. 'Leave her where she is until I get there.'

As we made our way slowly up the hill against the biting cold wind, I could see where she lay, her limbs paddling, with the sod worn off under her. A quick listen to the booming, rapid heartbeat confirmed my suspicions of grass tetany – a metabolic condition where the magnesium levels in the body drop, resulting in the collapse and neurological signs that lay before me. The problem with treating an animal in this condition was that any stress or excitement could trigger a seizure and instant death.

The first thing to do was to sedate her, so I drew up a small volume of sedative and slipping the needle into the vein, I depressed the plunger. Gradually, the laboured breathing of the cow became more relaxed and even.

Now I felt a little more confident and fitted the bottle of magnesium to the flutter valve and inserted the wide-bore needle under the skin. I flicked at the value and watched as the air bubbled up into the familiar brown bottle.

With the stethoscope in my ears, I carefully auscultated the heart, waiting for the familiar pattern to return. By the time the bottle had drained in and I was ready to add a bottle of calcium, this time directly into the vein, the tips of my finger had become numb and I fumbled to find the vein in the thickened, hairy groove. The cow moaned slightly and I stood up holding the bottle as high as the flutter valve would allow, speeding up the flow. As I was bending down again to recheck the heart, from behind the bush, I could see two lambs capering around the hill seemingly oblivious to the near Arctic conditions. A distinctive black patch over the flank assured me that the larger of the two was Gulliver, but it was hard to believe that he was only two weeks old.

'He's as fine a lamb as you'd ever see, isn't he, Tom?' I said, turning to face my companion who was wiping at the stream of tears that were whipped from his eyes by the wind, forming a thin trickle down his face.

'There's no doubt about that,' he replied. 'But what do ye think of the one beside him?'

In contrast to Gulliver, his playmate was not much to look at. The tiny lamb looked no more than a few days old and was poorly built. I was surprised at Tom drawing my attention to her, but didn't want to offend him, knowing how attached he and Mary were to their stock.

'A bit of sunshine on her back and she'll come on

nicely,' I replied, carefully, and wondered why my response caused Tom to break out in wheezy laugh as the stream of tears down his face thickened.

Before long I was happy that the cow was on the mend and we padded her up well with thickets of gorse to prop her into sternal position to allow her to get up more easily when the sedative had worn off.

Making our way back down the hill, Tom kept erupting into half-coughing, half-laughing fits and nodding his head wisely. I began to wonder if old age and harsh conditions were beginning to take their toll.

Mary had obviously spotted us making our way down the steep hill and was waiting at the back door to greet us.

'How's Bella?' she called out while we were still quite a distance away. A thumbs-up sign from me brought a smile of relief and she hurried back into the kitchen again. By the time I had packed my gear away in the car and come into the kitchen for a wash, the table was set with a pot of tea and hot scones.

'And I won't take no for an answer this time,' she told me firmly. Despite her dainty stature, I didn't dare argue.

Although the couple seemed in good form, in fact almost giddy at times, I felt that something strange was going on.

By the second scone, Mary burst out, obviously no longer able to contain herself, 'Well, what did you make of the twins up there?'

'The twins?' I enquired, puzzled, wondering which ones they was talking about.

'Gulliver and Lilly,' she said. 'I saw you looking at them up there.'

'Well, I was just saying to Tom what a fine lamb Gulliver is, but who does Lilly belong to?'

'Lilly is Gulliver's little sister,' cried Tom, triumphantly.

I stared at them both blankly, wondering what had come over them. Although it was not uncommon for a lamb from a ewe with multiple lambs to be fostered onto a ewe with a single, they surely wouldn't have fostered it onto Edel with a big lump like Gulliver to feed.

At this stage, the couple were falling around the table, in uncontrolled mirth, breaking up laughing every time they looked at my confused face.

'It was such a fine day, the day Gulliver arrived, that we decided to let himself and Edel out with the others,' began Tom, pausing to catch his breath every now and again. 'The next morning, I went out with George to feed them and down trotted Edel with Gulliver close behind. Well, I thought I was seeing things,' he continued, warming to the tale, 'because by the look of him he had six legs. When he got closer though, I was able to see that two of the legs belonged to a little speck of a lamb and while Edel was having her nuts, there the two of them were, feeding away from her, one on either side, like Little an Large.'

I stared at them in open-mouthed amazement. 'And where did she come from?' I asked stupidly, hoping I had missed a part of the story

'Well, Edel was the last due to lamb. Apart from the few hoggets in the far pen, all the rest had lambed. Sure, the poor little bugger must have been in there all along and watched the brother being pulled out and wondered what the hell was going on when you stitched her up again!'

My face must have gone deathly white as realisation dawned on me exactly what had happened before Mary quickly intervened.

'But sure, not to worry,' she cried, in obvious glee at the story. 'She was that tiny she slipped out the usual way, not a bother on her.'

Despite their obvious enjoyment of the story, I couldn't really share it with them. My mind was filled with horror, thinking back to the caesarean and my amazement at the size of the lamb and the unbroken history of a single, and wondering had I really not carried out the usual examination around the uterus to check for a second or even a third?

'But maybe,' I stammered, 'well, maybe, could one of the smaller hoggets have been in lamb and had it without you knowing?'

'Well, I suppose it's possible,' considered Tom, 'although I didn't see any signs of it.'

'And she always was a bossy ewe, Edel,' carried on Mary. 'She'd be just the one to decide the youngsters weren't doing it right and take over.'

And to this day, we don't know. Did Edel break the trend and have twin lambs, one with my help and the other despite my hindrance, or did she take a fancy to an inexperienced hogget's lamb?

CHAPTER TEN

BEAUTY – OR THE BEAST?

As usual, the week had rolled around to Wednesday night before I knew it, and I prepared myself for the weekly Blue Cross onslaught. At quarter to five I was sitting in a comfortable armchair trying to remind myself why I did it. The clients would have another good hour before they would have to get ready to go out in the fierce winds and the dark rain that I couldn't ignore, no matter how hard I tried, beating against the window. Not for the first time I wondered why the Blue Cross couldn't expand to having a clinic in Wicklow.

One look at my bag was enough for Molly to break into an agonised wail. 'Mammy, make sick doggies better – Monny coming too!'

'No, Molly stay and mind Sluggie,' I reassured her firmly. I was having more success with the Maltesers I placed in her sticky fist, and feeling totally unrepentant of the buy-off.

Slug drooled hopefully, waiting for the inevitable titbit.

The journey seemed to go in slow motion as I shivered despite the thin trickle of heat I allowed myself in the car – no point in warming up too much.

Surely on such a night there won't be a big crowd, I consoled myself, in a vain attempt at self-delusion. And a delusion it was. From the far side of the roundabout I could see the assortment of teenagers with puppies, and old men with old dogs and young women with shivering children and somewhere in their midst an equally shivering pet.

I noticed a forlorn-looking budgie hopping miserably from one perch to the next, despairing at the variety of natural predators that surrounded him.

'Right, let the budgie in first,' I called above the din, ignoring the good-humoured protest that broke out.

'So, what seems to be the problem?' I enquired of the equally bedraggled young girl, clutching the cage as though her life depended on it.

'Ah nuttin', Doc. I just brought 'im for ye to have a look at 'im.'

I looked at her closely, trying to see if she was winding me up, but the big innocent eyes gazing up trustingly at me gave nothing away.

Gently, I tried to explain to her how such tiny birds have fairly delicate hearts and that even my handling him could be enough to make him keel over. 'Budgies don't like any change – he hates that wind and rain, so get him home and cover his cage with a large towel and keep him quiet for the rest of the night,' I finished, praying to God that the little creature wouldn't be belly-up by that stage.

'Yeah, I know all dat, Doc,' she called back over her shoulder as Eamon carefully ushered her down the big steps, 'but de ye *like* 'im?'

I tried not to catch Gordon's eye as the crowd surged through the open door.

Soon I was in the thick of it – clients pushing in from both doors – examining one patient while shouting medication doses to Gordon for the previous case. My stethoscope hung idly by, to be used only when absolutely necessary; no self-respecting stethoscope could even hope to pick up on any pathology over the constant roar of the evening traffic, mulled together with the wails and squawks and roars of the assorted assembly of animal life with which we were surrounded.

Nearing the end of the first hour, I felt we were making progress until I glanced out into the tiny waiting area and my eyes were drawn to the most ominous of all signs: a man with a pillowcase on his lap.

Over the next vomiting kitten and Jack Russell for suture removal, I tried to push the image of that pillowcase to the back of my mind, but as the terrier jumped happily off the table into the arms of her owner, there it was – the pillowcase – dumped unceremoniously in front of me.

The pretty pink floral borders did nothing to fool me. For as long as I could, I put off the moment, trying to judge from the thick bulk of the contents just how bad it could be.

'A four-and-a-half-foot boa constrictor,' declared the man proudly as I hesitatingly enquired.

A gasp of breath came from behind me as a young woman, clutching a scrawny kitten and desperately trying to grasp the hands of her assortment of toddlers, shot out the door and, with a resounding slam, we were on our own – myself, the man, and the four-and-a-half-foot boa constrictor.

'Need a hand?' enquired Eamon, poking a head in the door.

'Emm, yeah. Sure. Come on in,' I answered, feeling in need of some moral support if nothing else.

The man seemed oblivious to my discomfort. 'A real beauty he is,' he began, his hand delving in among the pink printed flowers.

The reptilian smell assailed me before I even saw the head darting out, inquisitively flicking its forked tongue, assessing the situation.

'A real beauty,' he repeated, offering the muscular trunk towards me as I involuntarily stepped back almost falling into the press behind me, the pointed head a little too close for comfort.

'So, em, what exactly seems to be the problem, then?' I enquired, hastily pulling on a rare pair of disposable gloves and reminding myself of the oath in which we swore to care for all creatures, slithery or not!

Oblivious to the still considerable crowd outside, Freddie enthusiastically launched into the tale of how a mate of his had bought this snake from a pet shop, despite the fact that his wife wasn't keen on it. Apparently, one evening, the snake had escaped from its enclosure and while the non-reptile-fancying wife was taking a bath, she spied the tail-end of it coiled neatly behind the toilet bowl.

'Well, jeepers, me mate said ye'd want te have heard the

roars outa her. She wouldn't have yer man in the house after that,' he finished, nodding towards the mottled reptile winding its way up his arm.

'Strange that,' I murmured faintly, feeling deep sympathy for the unfortunate woman.

'So, he's just in for a check-up then?' I implored hopefully, wondering if I could conceivably go through the motions of examining the creature without touching it, even through Latex-lined hands.

'Well no, luv,' he replied, dashing all hopes. 'I've had the bugger for about two weeks now and 'e hasn't eaten at all. I've offered 'im the best of grub – got a few live chicks an' all – wouldn't look at them.'

I shuddered, imagining myself as the luckless chick.

Frantically, I racked my brains wondering how often a four-and-a-half-foot boa constrictor should eat. Two weeks did seem a bit long, but not totally famine-length either.

From my vantage point, the creature's scales did seem to be a bit dry and lifeless, but there was nothing lifeless about the rest of it as, with remarkable speed and agility, he slithered around Freddie's body, coiling and wrapping as best he knew.

'Well, maybe he's taking a bit of time settling into his new environment?' I began, buying myself a bit of time. 'He does look a bit dehydrated and, with the stress of the move, he's not shedding his coat properly,' I continued, feeling a little more confident that this ordeal would come to an end soon. 'What I would do is give him a bath in lukewarm water every second day to rehydrate him and syringe a bit of this into him after it,' I replied, scribbling down the name of a reptile food supplement which would be available in the pet shop.

'That should get him back on his feet,' I concluded, missing the point that he didn't have any, and now frantic to conclude the consultation.

Freddie seemed happy enough with that. 'Right, luv. I'll do that so and, sure, if he's not eating I'll bring 'im back to ye again.'

I mumbled something that was not quite confirmatory but was feeling that I had got away lightly. Thankfully, I pulled off the still-clean pair of gloves, but Freddie turned back towards me and as an afterthought added, 'But are ye sure he 'asn't gotta touch o' mouth rot?' he said, thrusting the serpentine head towards mine. For an instant our eyes locked in mutual distrust before I recovered enough to pull myself away.

'Well, eh, I don't really think so,' I said cautiously as though X-ray specks were allowing me to examine the content of the mouth that was firmly latched shut.

'Would ye like me te open 'is mouth for ye?'

Maybe it was finally beginning to dawn on Freddie that I wasn't as enamoured of his 'beauty' as he was.

'Yes, good idea, so,' I blustered. 'I wouldn't like to frighten him.'

I studiously ignored Eamon's amused raised eyebrow as, taking a deep breath, I managed to peer into the gaping, one hundred and eighty degree jaws that were presented to me. Feeling a bit like that poor chick in its final moments, I could see clearly enough that the mouth area was thankfully clear of infections that would require my intervention.

'Perfect, perfect,' I assured Freddie, hastily opening the door for the next client as he coiled his companion back into the floral print pillowcase.

Three or four clients had passed through before I could swallow without a gulp and the skin on the back of my neck stopped feeling quite so clammy.

'Was tha' a snake ye had in de bag?' asked one enthusiastic young lad. 'Deadly. Bleedin' deadly!' he said when I confirmed that it was.

'Yeah … deadly,' I agreed, shuddering again.

On the long drive home I kept getting a shivery feeling down my spine and I did have a quick peek around the interior of the car before I got in. That night, I kept the duvet well wrapped around me, making sure there were no cracks and when Molly woke for her usual bottle, instead of running across the hall in my bare feet, I put on a pair of heavy duty slippers … just in case.

The following Wednesday night came and went and although there was the usual assortment of life, there were no pink pillowcases. I breathed a sigh of relief when the last fluffy kitten had left.

I had all but forgotten my ordeal when, two weeks later, just as we were finishing up well beyond the allocated time as usual, Eamon called after me, 'Hang on a sec, there's someone after getting off that bus. Will we wait for them?'

'Oh all right, so,' I replied grudgingly, wondering who else would have arrived by the time we dealt with this one.

'What is it?' I called out the door, wondering what I needed to unpack.

Silence.

Eamon sounded sheepish when he came back in. 'Are you sure you want to look at his one? We are well over time. We could always get him to come back next week or he could even go to Walkinstown tomorrow night. I'll be on that clinic myself and I'm sure we could look after him there.'

I eyed him suspiciously – Eamon wasn't usually prone to rambling, long night or not.

'Sure, it'll only take us a minute, Eamon. Call him in there.'

It struck me just before I saw it, this time not in a pink but in a yellow pillowcase, adorned with fluffy teddy bears. The beauty was back.

I flinched, as with a thump, the encased body hit the table.

'No joy, luv. No joy at all,' declared Freddie gloomily.

I couldn't but agree with him.

'We didn't see you last week. I assumed all was well,' I said with forced enthusiasm.

'Nah, I tried to get over to ye but the bleedin' bus was late and by the time I got here yiz were gone.'

'Well, the clinic is only meant to be from seven to eight,' pointed out Gordon, looking at his watch which showed that it was now looming dangerously close to nine. 'You're lucky that we're still here at all – we should be sitting down in front of our fires by now.'

'Ah thanks, lads,' Freddie replied automatically. 'It's jus' tha' he hasn't eaten at all since the last time and I've been doing me best, I have. Gave 'im a wash like yiz said.'

Despite myself, I felt sorry for the creature as Freddie pulled it out of the bag. The previously thick, muscular trunk looked gaunt and saggy and the skin was thickly scaled and dry. Even his movements were weak and list-less, and he was apparently uninterested in his fate, as his head hung, barely level with the rest of his body. He was clearly a very sick snake and far beyond my feeble attempts at this stage. With a sense of relief, and knowing I was doing the right thing, I told Freddie that a referral to an exotics clinic was the only answer at this stage.

A long conversation ensued during which Freddie related his saga of how he had no means of transport to get across to the far side of the city and being on welfare he couldn't afford to pay much, and sure, anyway, the missus was getting fed up with the snake in the sitting room. After almost two hours at the clinic, my powers of persuasion were at their lowest ebb and with a sense of doom, I could feel what was coming next.

By quarter past nine, Freddie was gone and only the teddy-bear pillowcase remained behind, complete with my new in-patient. Beauty or not, Freddie had baled out.

Much and all as I feared the beast, I couldn't bring myself to put him to sleep. I wasn't concerned about get-ting a home for him as there are lots of people who like this kind of pet; but getting him better was going to be more difficult, plus the more immediate problem of what to do with him tonight.

Gordon and Eamon didn't even allow me to air my

brainwave that perhaps one of them would like a new pet.

'No, no,' Gordon assured me. 'What he needs now is a nice drive in the country. Nothing like a bit of fresh air to work up an appetite!'

The pair of them erupted into laughter at my desolate face.

I tried to bargain with myself, using all my logic. My phobia for snakes was ridiculous – pure childhood prejudice. Maybe this was my chance to break it. Maybe, in caring for this seriously ill animal, I would begin to bond with the species and get a better feel for them. Really, it was an excellent opportunity for me.

I wasn't convinced, but there was no other option and anyway, I told myself, he's so sick what harm can he do?

We got halfway home – as far as the canal – in relative tranquility, with Sidney, as I had christened him, hoping to make him seem friendlier, quietly coiled in his pillowcase on the passenger seat. The smell of reptile was growing, whether in my mind or in reality I'm not sure, so I opened the window to let in some Dublin fumes to overpower it. However, at the next bridge, it suddenly occurred to me that if he did escape he might make for the open crack, straight across my lap. Quickly, I closed the window again.

With one eye on the road and the other on the inert pillowcase, I drove on, trying to ignore the prickling sensation up the back of my neck. I was just crossing a busy intersection over the canal when, suddenly, I caught sight of the whole pillowcase rearing up and lurching towards me over the gear stick. In synchronicity with my body, the car swerved over the white line, amidst blasts of horns, while a cyclist skidded into the footpath. The edge of the pillowcase was touching my leg, and part of the dense body of the snake had fallen down between the seat and the gear stick. With a shaking hand, I managed to pick the pillowcase up by the very edge and flick it back onto the seat while trying to get the car back into the correct lane.

The feeling of claustrophobia was growing in intensity with every passing mile. At the next junction, while waiting for the lights to change, I heard the gentle hissing sound, almost like the air being let out of a tyre. Through the well-worn material, I could see the outline of his head, upright, obviously as unimpressed with me as I was with him. At this stage I decided, for the sake of my fellow road users as much as myself, that Sidney would be better off in the boot. With the hazard lights flashing, I gingerly picked up the bag, and trying to ignore the still considerable weight of four-and-a-half feet of emaciated constrictor, I placed him gently in the boot, wedged between my vet bag and Molly's spare clothes bag, hoping she wouldn't object to the invasion.

My relief was short-lived. Out onto the Donnybrook road and there it was again … I was sure, ever so faint, but surely that was the hissing noise again? With an indignant squeal, the car slammed to a halt and I jumped out, wondering how he had managed to escape. But when I checked the boot, there was no change. His dark silhouette was still where I had left it.

Back in car and this time I tried turning on the radio to drown out my over-active imagination. I flicked from my usual East Coast Radio until I hit the soothing notes of Lyric. I managed as far as Stillorgan before turning down the volume and listening: nothing. And again: still nothing. Was he just silent or had he escaped – and was he, right now, at this moment, making his way up over the back seat towards me …?

That's it, I thought to myself. Enough of this! I got out to reclaim Sidney from the boot. Back he went to the passenger side, but this time onto the floor where he couldn't move about as much.

We got as far as Cabinteely and in disbelief I stared at the long line of traffic ahead of me. At a quarter to ten at night, this could only mean one thing.

'Oh, why tonight?' I groaned. 'Of all nights to have a police checkpoint.' Mentally, I checked my tax and insurance and readjusted my safety belt.

'Now, you just stay there and don't move,' I threatened the pillowcase.

With the car slowed in the bumper-to-bumper queue, the smell seemed to get worse. When it was finally my turn to roll down the window, I was sure the guard couldn't miss the stench.

'Good evening, Miss,' drawled the guard with the tones of a man who was clearly not in a hurry.

Having caught up on the vital information of who I was and where I was going, he made his way in carefully measured steps to the windscreen and pointedly examined the discs, which were, thankfully, all in order. Just as he peered in the windscreen, Sidney, obviously getting bored with it all, started his antics again, tossing his head high within the constraint of his pillowcase as though trying to get back up on the seat.

'Be quiet,' I hissed at him, not knowing why as I didn't think it was illegal to be carrying a snake around, but still, it was easier not to have to explain.

The guard frowned and with chest expanded and shoulders raised as though on the verge of making an important breakthrough, he came back to the driver's window again and pushed his head in towards me.

'May I ask who you were addressing, Miss?' he asked in exaggerated monotones.

'Who? Me? Oh, no one at all, Guard,' I replied, my voice a bit high. 'Just talking to myself, you know. Lonely drive on a late night, and all that.'

He peered at me through narrowed eyes and then casting his glance around the car, came across the pillowcase tied firmly in a knot on the floor.

'And what have you got in the pillowcase?'

'Oh, that?' I said, voice rising again in forced gaiety. 'Not much at all, Sir. Just a boa constrictor.'

His head shot back out the window and he stood upright again.

'Do you know, Miss, that it is an offence to hinder the work of a member of the Garda Siochána?'

'Really? Gosh, no! I never knew that. Wouldn't dream of it though, your honour. Would you like to have a look?'

With perfect timing, Sidney made another strike, this time as though trying to execute the perfect back flip. The bag flopped over and, with an audible thump, hit off the passenger door.

I looked up, waiting for the guard to reply but, with a loud bang on my roof, he beckoned me on, only pausing to add, 'The left front tyre is a bit bald,' as though I had committed a grievous felony.

I finally made it home in one piece and walked in the door to where Donal was peacefully watching a video.

'What's the pillowcase for?' he enquired.

'You won't believe it. But there was nothing I could do. I really had no option.'

With a sense of accustomed bewilderment he took the bag from me and opened it up to take a look inside, not noticing I had backed up against the far wall.

'Is it still alive?' I tried to quell the hope that rose within me.

'Oh it is,' he said, quickly closing the bag as Sidney obviously decided to introduce himself.

It took a while to get my old vivarium down out of the attic. Despite my aversion to snakes, I quite like lizards and had kept a pair of Bearded Dragons for many years. Luckily, their vivarium was still intact and although the ultraviolet light needed a new plug, the heat pads were all in perfect working order. Although the vivarium came complete with a solid, fitted lid with appropriate air holes, I placed the *Irish Times Atlas of the World* and a few other hefty volumes on top, just to be sure.

There was nothing more to be done with Sidney at that hour of the night, so having given him a spray of lukewarm water to make sure the humidity was right, we headed wearily to bed.

It took a while before I fell into a fitful slumber, working out the list of names I would ring in the morning to organise a new home for Sidney as quickly as possible.

*   *   *

It was the early hours of the morning before my disturbed dreams were interrupted by a loud banging noise and a heavy thump. In a panic, my first though was that Molly had fallen out of her cot and I leapt out, forgetting all about our house guest. When I raced into Molly's room, there she lay, sleeping peacefully, covers thrown to one side but still clutching the furry cow that joined her each night. With a start, I remembered about the snake and looked down warily at my bare feet.

I walked cautiously through the rooms to try to find out what had made the noise. When I reached the sitting-room, I saw that a pile of books and assorted junk had fallen out of the large press which was home to any odds and ends that didn't fit anywhere else in the house. I had ransacked it earlier, looking for the heaviest possible books to put on top of Sidney's vivarium. With a sigh of relief, I started to stuff the collection back into the press.

In the silence of that hour of the morning, it was unmistakable – a loud hissing noise came from the back of the press. With a scream which might well have been audible in Ballyfermot, some forty miles away, I woke the household. In an instant, Slug and the other four dogs charged in, ready and able to defend me against anything. They were followed closely by Donal, just as Molly's bewildered wails broke out over the general confusion.

'The snake is in the press,' I yelled hysterically at Donal. 'He's hissing at me.' I stopped short as my eyes fell on the vivarium where Sidney was clearly visible through the glass, sleeping peacefully, neatly coiled and oblivious to the pandemonium he was creating.

'But he was, he was hissing at me in the press when I pushed the books back in,' I told Donal, relieved and yet confused as to what had happened.

And even though we could still see Sidney, as calm grew there *was* a hissing noise.

'Have a look,' I urged Donal. 'I'll go and get Molly.'

By the time I got back with Molly in my arms, sobs now reduced to a sleepy snuffle, Donal was laughing, a can of air freshener in his hand which I vaguely remembered from three or four years back when we were trying to sell our old house and get rid of the dog smell. It seemed that the can had been lying in the press with the lid off and when I had pushed the books in, the spray nozzle had jammed and hence the hissing noise.

My laughter was as much nervous relief as general amusement over the whole situation. I have to admit that I've never been too fond of aerosols since.

A few hours later, I got out my phone book and started ringing the four or five contacts I had who had an interest in reptiles, eager to pass on Sidney before the serious work had to be done. Reptile fanciers in general tend to be passionate about their hobby, so I was quite sure that one of them would be happy to take him on in his current condition. And most of them were far more knowledgeable than I would ever be in relation to the creatures. But luck was not on my side. I was on my last hope, but Dieter, a German living in North Dublin, although keen, was going away for a week that very morning. If I could keep Sidney until his return ...? I had no choice. Seven long days before I could hand him over – if he lasted that long.

Clearly, the previous night's exertions had taken their toll on Sidney. That morning he appeared quite lifeless, coiled neatly around a log I had left for him in the vivarium. I checked both the temperature and humidity and satisfied myself that both were suitable and started reading up my reptile book.

Apart from his obvious ill-health, the only other clinical signs were the telltale bubbles that appeared over his nostril at regular intervals. This was indicative of some form of respiratory infection, but whether this was secondary to his ill health or the initiating factor, I didn't know.

What he needed was a daily injection of antibiotics, regular bathing in tepid water and worst of all, stomach tubing, to force some essential nutrients into the reluctant feeder. All of this I had done before, but usually at a clinic where the owner was able to hold the snake while I performed the tasks with carefully gloved hands.

Molly was clearly enthralled with the newcomer when she saw him first.

'Nicey snakey,' she cooed at him. 'Monny hold him?' she questioned, inquisitive eyes looking up at me.

'No, no! Don't touch!' I replied, a little too abruptly. 'He's too sick,' I added. 'But he is a very nice snake,' I assured her, not wanting to pass on my phobia.

In order to calculate the correct dose of the medications, Sidney had to weighed. Although I could quite accurately estimate the weight of a cat or a dog by picking them up, I had not handled enough snakes to even begin to estimate his weight. I had to get him back into his pillowcase – last night, it had seemed relatively easy to tip him out of the pillowcase into the carefully prepared vivarium, but now, how I wished I had left him where he was. Pulling on my gloves, I braced myself, reached down and cautiously touched the smooth body. The warmth always took me by surprise. The problem was that his head was tucked down in the middle of the coil so I couldn't get hold of it. Trying to make things easier, I decided that maybe I would be able to slip the pillowcase under him and scoop him into it without any major handling. Slowly, gradually, I eased the frayed edge in under the coil, but when I was almost half way there, the head suddenly shot up as though he was only now realising the unwelcome intrusion. I dropped the pillowcase and jumped up, almost knocking Molly over as she stood close by, delighted with the morning's entertainment.

Obviously weakened by his prolonged illness, Sidney's head drooped again. Taking a deep breath and quelling the waves of nausea that were threatening to overcome me, I managed to grasp him just behind the head – firmly, but gently enough not to damage the delicate bones in the area. I shuddered as he squirmed in my hands, but kept my hold, more afraid now of letting him go. With one eye firmly fixed on him, I reached over for the pillowcase and gradually drew him up high enough to drop his tail end into it. Once his bulk was safely contained, I let go of his head, withdrew my hand and held my breath for a few moments until all was still. Keeping a firm hold on the top,

I sat him up on the weighing scales and at last, the first task was completed.

Dropping pillowcase and all back into the vivarium, I was able to calculate and draw up the correct dose of anti-biotic in the tiny insulin syringe. I contemplated injecting him through the bag but figured it would be better to know where the head was. I rolled back the edges until he was sitting on top of it, and, grasping the head, edged the needle in under the skin between two scales. With almost a sense of sympathy, I noticed how thin and gaunt he was, but was relieved that in his weakened state he didn't even seem to notice my ministrations.

The next task was the bath. With Sidney safely con-tained in his pillowcase, I went in search of a suitable con-tainer. Search as I did, though, I failed to come up with anything suitable for a four-and-a-half-foot constrictor to have a bath in. There was nothing for it – our own bath it would have to be.

Molly clapped her hands when she saw me running a mix of hot and cold water into the bath and immediately started pulling off her fleecy jumper.

'Monny bath! Monny bath!' she cried, in obvious glee at the unexpected morning treat.

'No, Molly. The bath is for the snake.'

She looked at me incredulously and I couldn't but agree with her – maybe I was losing it.

With ten centimetres of tepid water gently swirling around the bath, I slowly lowered the snake. It wasn't until he sank down to the bottom that I began to wonder if he would know to hold his head up over the water level or not.

I counted to five as he lay motionless below the surface, thin trails of bubbles blowing out of his nostrils. There was nothing for it but reach down and grasp the head.

So there I knelt, crouching over the bath, firmly holding Sidney's head at arm's length and watching, with a mix of horror and fascination, as the long body gradually relaxed and uncoiled and lazily flicked from side to side, creating little whirlpools in the water.

Of course, the phone had to ring.

Desperately trying to get my mobile out of my right pocket with my left hand while keeping my eyes fixed on Sidney, I finally managed to hold it up to my ear. It was the bank manager. If I was free, he asked, could I take a few minutes to discuss my account with him? Glad of the excuse, I casually informed him that I was actually tied up at the moment – bathing a snake.

Sounding slightly incredulous, he began to enquire as to why I was bathing a snake. Then, out of the corner of my eye, I spotted Molly, who had been strangely quiet up to now, heaving a large bottle of bubble bath up onto the edge of the bath.

'Snakey like bubbles. Pink bubbles!' she declared as she started to tip the contents into the bath water.

'No, Molly!' I shouted and I reached out to grab it from her while still holding onto Sidney. I watched in horror as the phone slipped out of my hands, skidded along the edge of the bath tub and with a resounding plop, fell into the water.

I didn't even begin to wonder what the bank manager would think – but at least he couldn't ring me back, I thought wistfully, as I watched my phone glide carelessly up and down along the base of the bath from the current created by Sidney's body.

'Okay. That will have to do you,' I told Sidney after what seemed a lot longer than fifteen minutes.

All that was left to do now was to stomach tube him with the mix of concentrate feed and supplements, specifically designed for ailing reptiles. I was well familiar with the scenario of having the snake restrained by the owner, with the first half metre or so, depending on the size, dangling down vertically, to allow me to slip the carefully measured tube over the back of the mouth and down into the stomach. Today, with no loving owner to console him, Sidney was in no mood to cooperate. Clearly in a huff at being hauled out of the warm bath, he was now coiled tightly in a roll with only the head that I was still holding, sticking out.

Obstinately, he refused to open his mouth, which I gently probed with the well lubricated tip of a stomach tube.

There was nothing for it but to lower him back into the bath to see if he would uncoil. It took three or four more attempts before I finally managed to get him to open his mouth so I could pass the tube in. He hung down, the bottom few feet still in the bath water. With the stomach tube in place, he hung sullenly, obviously reluctant to coil with the rubber tube in him. With one hand, I managed to attach the sixty millilitre syringe onto the top of the tube and gently squirt in the mushy, grey-brown liquid.

I watched the last of it disappear down the tube with the

aid of gravity, but before it had all gone down, Sidney decided to rebel. Flicking his tail up again, with the skill of a well practised contortionist, he began to coil. Dropping the syringe, I was forced to grab him mid-trunk and resist against the surprisingly powerful movements to keep him in a straight line, until all the fluid had trickled in. I tried to ignore the muscular rippling under my hands until I was satisfied that the tube was empty and I could safely remove it.

'Right. That's it. You're done!' I said, thankful at last to be able to release the head and drop him back into the vivarium before firmly replacing the lid.

The next week seemed to rotate around injections, baths and tube-feeding as it took a few hours each day to muster up the courage to approach my patient. By day three, the bubbles had stopped blowing out his nostril and when I reweighed him on day five, despite myself, I was pleased to see that he had put on some weight. By the end of the week, the previously dull skin was starting to shed and the thin backbone was not quite so visible. I felt confident that Sidney was beginning on the long road to recovery – I just didn't know how long it would take. My main problem now was that as Sidney recovered his strength, he became livelier and more aware of my limitations as a snake handler. While he loved his bath and tolerated his injections, I could no longer tube him on my own. As soon as he would see the tube coming, he would coil himself firmly into a knot, knowing full well that I wouldn't have the ability to force him out of it. By the sixth day, I offered Donal the option of holding his trunk or passing the stomach tube. Thankfully, he chose the former as I was much more confident at giving out directions than following them.

On the following Thursday morning, after Sidney had survived my tender, if not so loving care for a full week, the phone rang.

I was never more relieved to hear Dieter's German accent booming down the line. He was aware of my reluctance with his beloved species, and he could never quite comprehend it.

'But surely, you vill vant to keep him now you have made him better?' he questioned.

'Oh no, he's all yours,' I assured him quickly. 'How soon do you think you can get here?'

So keen was Dieter to see his new charge that he insisted on making a detour from Dublin airport via Wicklow. By the time he arrived, I had all the medications and instructions packed. The only thing that remained was Sidney himself, who seemed to be a little feisty this morning. Graciously, I allowed Dieter the honour of loading his new addition.

'Doesn't look too bad now, does he?' admired Dieter, as Sidney looped himself in slow, gracious movements up his arms and around his neck in a casual manner that he had never displayed with me.

Despite the mutual love-hate relationship that I had built up with Sidney, I was very relieved to see him being loaded into the back of the Ford Fiesta. As soon as the crunching of gravel stopped, I packed up all the containers, stomach tubes, heat pads and the whole array of accessories that he had used and soaked them in a strong disinfectant solution in the bath. That evening, having drained and dried all the accessories, I disinfected the bath, scrubbing it as it had never been scrubbed before. To this day, I still, personally, prefer to use the shower!

I was a bit surprised not to hear from Dieter over the next few days, but no news was most definitely good news in this case.

A few weeks later, just when the nightmares were beginning to fade and I was almost feeling brave enough to sleep with my feet sticking out from under the duvet, an A4 envelope arrived, lined on one side with stiff cardboard. Eagerly I ripped it open and to my horror, out fell a photograph of Sidney in mid-strike, jaws opened one hundred and eighty degrees wide around the scrawny body of a day-old chick. In horror, I dropped it, the quality of the photograph being so good that I could almost smell him again. The sheet enclosed read:

To Gillian.
As you can see the snake is now back to full health and eating well. Thanks again,
Dieter.
PS 'Sidney' is a female – have decided to call her Beauty.

CHAPTER ELEVEN

A DIFFERENT
CONSULTATION

L ooking at the appointment book for tomorrow, I shuddered in horror. The morning would be taken up with an obese Labrador spay, followed by a messy TB test in a bachelor farmer's pad, where organisation wouldn't be the outstanding quality of the operation. But, for once, these didn't worry me. What was causing my anguish was the afternoon appointment: 3.30pm: Gillian – annual accountant meeting.

Already I could picture myself meandering through the morning's work, hoping that if I stalled long enough I could, justifiably, ring and postpone, knowing, however, that on the one morning that I wanted Terry Byrne to be his usual, disorganised self, he would have his meagre stock in perfect order. I mentally packed the two Solpadine which I could take before heading off to the brightly coloured office of the accountant, where, deceptively, real plants actually grew. However, the bright décor and living plants was where it all ended. Once trapped inside the four walls, I knew there would be no escape from the mental torture that lay ahead.

It had started some two months before when the odd memo had begun to appear in the day book: Gillian – call accountant. The next month: Gillian – accountant looking for files. Some weeks later: Gillian – accountant missing statements. On they went.

Although working within a practice, like most mixed animal practitioners I remained self-employed – a ploy, it seemed, devised to ensure the prosperity of accountants for many generations to come. I actually thought that I was quite good at my end of things, meticulously filling in cheque stubs, filing invoices of paid and unpaid dockets, putting all the bank statements in one designated folder, even remembering to file the grey, not the blue copy of the chemist's prescription (remembering grey for accountant – boring). However, despite my best efforts, the invisible goblin that seemed, on an annual basis, to accompany my carefully sorted accounts from our house to the account-ant's office somehow managed to delete files, mix up paid and unpaid invoices, eliminate whole cheque-book stubs – anything that could cause general chaos.

I soon discovered that going to the accountant was a bit like going to the doctor. Once you got inside, the exchang-ing of pleasantries, possibly designed to settle your nerves, inevitably served only to prolong the suspense. Once that was over (having probably added a significant amount to the bill) it was on to the nitty gritty of things.

'On the twelfth of November you wrote a cheque for an undisclosed sum: explain!'

It was like being back at the oral exams in college but, in reality, I was more likely to be able to explain the fertility problem of a maiden mare than to come up with any logical explanation as to why there was no record of my VAT return for some particular two-month period.

On the day in question, at the appointed hour, I genuinely tried to focus, tried to show some interest in what was going to account for a significant percentage of my annual expenditure. As the besuited figure at the opposite side of the table pushed a few obscure figures around an A4 pad, I glanced around me, staring in bewilderment at the rows of dull-coloured books in various poses around the office. A few opened pages – rows of figures, formulae, percentages and deductions – not a single clinical sign or surgical instrument in sight. I wondered, yet again, how anyone could spend their life in this environment.

On it dragged – more putting this into petty cash, more writing this in and writing that off. If they can write things off like that, why can't I just make it all up, I wondered idly to myself?

The accountant, seeming oblivious to my mental anguish, was still enthusiastically wading through the file. Was I happy with this figure, or that total? he asked on a few occasions. Dumbly, I nodded, acutely aware that by the time he would get to the end of each lengthy explanation, I would have totally forgotten what we were discussing in the first place. Almost an hour into the meeting, while going through the tax allowances for purchasing surgical equipment, I almost felt that by the end of the lecture, I had some faint inkling of what he was talking about. As this was the first time during the session that this had happened, I asked what I hoped might be a semi-intelligent question, hoping to indicate some level of enthusiasm. He paused momentarily, looking surprised, as this was the first sentence I had uttered with more than monosyllables. Within seconds, I realised my mistake. Enthused by my tiny little flickering spark of potential interest, he was off, launching into a verbal explosion of molten lava which was no more use than dry ash by the time it got to my ears. It reminded me of the time I had started to spay a bitch helped by a student on her first day seeing practice. Enthused by her initial interest, I was happy to explain the surgical procedure in minute detail, pulling up a ligament or a uterine horn to demonstrate as I went along. It wasn't until fifteen minutes later that I noticed she had gone a bit grey. I caught hold of her just as she slumped silently to the floor.

As the accountant came to the end of his flow, I wondered, idly, what would happen if I passed out – would that get me out of the remainder of the meeting or would he just carry on over my semi-conscious body?

Thankfully, at that moment the phone rang. Apologising for the interruption, I answered. It was Joe Hartigan, an eighty-suckler cow farmer from Roundwood. I had calved a cow for him early that morning before going to the surgery. He had just checked her to find she had since prolapsed her uterus, or as he put it himself, 'put out her calf bed'.

'When did she put it out?' I asked him.

'Well, I'm just up from the lunch and she was all right when I left so it can't be out long now.'

'Is she up or down?' I further enquired.

'She's up at the moment, but she's gone a bit staggery, like. I wouldn't bet on her staying up for long.'

Joe was one of that generation firmly convinced that you needed to shout on the phone to be heard all that distance away. As I held the mobile even further from my ear, I noticed that the figure-fumbling at the other side of the desk had ceased and that the accountant was casting an occasional curious glance in my direction, obviously able to hear every word.

'Try and keep her up and keep it clean so she won't do any damage to the calf bed,' I advised him. 'If you wouldn't mind giving the office a ring, either Seamus or Arthur will be out to you in no time. I'm just tied up myself at the moment.'

'Right so, I'll do that then,' he bellowed down the phone.

Once the ringing in my ears had died down, the accountant tentatively asked, 'How could a cow do damage to the bed of a calf?'

'Well, if she goes down, it could tear or get dirty,' I answered, grateful to be on to a more familiar topic.

'But, isn't the bed just made up of straw and that?' he questioned, still clearly bewildered.

Gently I explained to him that the calf bed to which the farmer was referring was, in fact, the bed of the calf inside the cow and not outside.

His colour faded slightly, before he continued in a somewhat faint voice, 'But how does the "thing",' he paused, as though unable to refer to it by name, 'get out?'

'If the cow forces too hard, particularly if she's an older cow and has had a lot of calves or if it's a very big calf, it's easy for the whole uterus to pop out,' I explained. 'And, you see, once it's out,' I continued, warming to my topic, 'the blood supply gets trapped, so if you don't get it back in quickly you can be in trouble.'

'And how big is this thing?' he queried.

'Well, when it comes out fresh it's about this big,' I told him holding my hands wide apart, 'but, if that one's left until tonight it could get this big,' I assured him, throwing my hands very far apart to indicate the size of some of the engorged uteruses I have had the misfortune to try to replace.

'And you just ... push it back in ... the hole it came out?' he asked finally, having taken some moments to assimilate the information.

'Yeah, something like that,' I agreed uncertainly, suddenly realising he wasn't quite ready for a full-blown pathology lecture.

'And you do *that* for a living?' he stated.

'And you do *this* for a living?' I replied.

There was silence for a few moments as we eyeballed each other – two aliens meeting in a hostile planet.

The stand-off was interrupted as the mobile rang again. It was the same number as before. 'Are you okay, Joe?' I asked, remembering to hold the phone a good foot from my ear to prevent permanent damage.

'Well, now, I've been trying to get Seamus but he isn't answering his phone. I was wondering if ye could come out yourself.'

In a flash it came to me that Arthur had had a late-night caesarean in Joe's yard which had turned out badly, and since then, even though Arthur was in no way at fault, Joe was reluctant to have him out.

'I can't come out to you now, Joe,' I replied, somewhat impatiently, knowing that the cow's chances were worsening the longer we delayed and also knowing that Arthur was a more experienced vet than me anyway. 'You'll have to get Arthur. I'm in a meeting with my accountant in Dublin at the moment.'

'You're meetin' the accountant!' he roared. 'Divil a bit o' good them lads will do ye. Ye'd be better off putting the few bob in your own back pocket than in theirs.'

I ended the call as quickly as I could but, although the accountant didn't comment, I had to suppress the occasional giggle as we crawled tediously though the negligible fixed and current assets.

By the time we got to page four of the accounts, I was starting to feel light-headed. I wasn't used to sitting still for such a long period of time and I was getting fidgety. I nodded brightly at appropriate intervals, knowing that my only escape was when I could finally sign off along the dotted line on page six.

Finally, it came to the end. Wearily, I scrawled my well-used signature along the indicated dotted line, more suited to signing cattle TB cards in the hundred than for a tidy little official document. The accountant signed his own name under mine, in fine flowing script. I couldn't help noticing his fine-skinned hand and even nails in comparison to my own.

Before bolting, I remembered that the accountant of the practice had asked me to ask him for some form to do with retention tax for TB testing. It sounded like such a vague, useless thing that I was sure the accountant would never have heard of it.

After a few attempts trying to explain what I was supposed to be looking for, he brightened up and started to rummage through a well used file. 'I have it here, I'm sure,' he said. 'Form P45 for PSWT deducted under Chapter 1 Part 19 of the 1997 Act' – he rattled off the long title, like a mantra.

I looked at him incredulously for a moment, and then the penny dropped. I broke into laughter, enjoying the chance to break the long tension. I was glad to see, despite it all, that he still had some vestige of a sense of humour.

He looked back at me, puzzled for a moment, and then flicked open a page. 'There it is,' he declared. 'Sorry, it's Part 18, not 19. I haven't looked at it for a while.'

Horrified, I realised that he wasn't joking. Turning my laugh into yet another cough, I nodded weakly as he offered to e-mail a copy to the practice accountant.

On the way home, I rang Donal.

'Well, how did it go?' he asked sympathetically.

'Oh, as expected,' I replied. 'Usual story. Made no money. Spent money we never had. Still more tax to pay and another few grand to pay him for the pleasure of his services.'

Donal's groan echoed mine down the phone.

'I'll get a take-away on the way home,' I offered, feeling we needed some sort of consolation.

'I'll put some Bulmer's in the fridge,' he replied.

'Had he anything useful to suggest,' Donal asked later as we dished out the chicken curry and listened to Slug noisily crunching the last of the prawn crackers.

'Well, apart from the fact that he thinks I should go for a career change altogether,' I told him, giggling, as I relayed the story of Joe and his calf bed. 'Other than that,' I continued, 'the usual stuff – buy stuff we don't need to save tax even though we don't have anything to buy it with. I think I'm supposed to go and lease a jeep or something and save loads of money.'

'That might not be the worst thing to do,' advised Donal. 'At least you'd have a bit of comfort getting around the farms and that. Much safer driving with Molly in the car too,' he added, warming to the idea.

'Ah sure, the banger will go on for a while yet, 'I replied, referring to the clapped-out Opel Corsa I had driven since I qualified. 'Anyway, Slug wouldn't be able to get in and out of a jeep with her dodgy legs.'

The conversation was interrupted as the phone rang. I answered it tentatively, hoping not to have to go out to anything major while my brain was still fried.

'Did you have a rough time?' Arthur announced himself, knowing my aversion to accountants.

'What do you think?' I replied glumly.

'Well. If it's any consolation, my day wasn't great either. I had to go out to old Joe Hartigan. He said you were out there this morning.'

'Oh. That's right. He was on to me too,' I replied, not mentioning the fact that he didn't want to get Arthur out.

'Well, you know the last night I was out there that cow died after the section and he thinks I'm the worst in the world? Well, this time, the cow had prolapsed. Uterus didn't look too bad, mind you. But the cow was down, very weak. In hindsight, she must have ruptured a blood vessel inside. I gave her the epidural and was rolling her around to get the hind legs back and didn't she give one great big bellow and drop dead!'

CHAPTER TWELVE

THE FILLY FOAL

The first time I ever encountered the Murphy clan was on a cold morning in early spring on my way to Riverside Clinic. I had just driven past their halting site when I came across a heavy piebald cob making her way along the grass verge at a lazy trot. The rhythmic swaying of her tense abdomen confirmed that she was in foal. From her well-worn halter trailed a long length of blue rope, which I assumed had once served to tether her. I pulled in to watch, surprised to find the creature loose, and wondered what had spooked her. I hesitated for a moment and then, with the car wedged into the ditch, I flicked on the hazard lights and hopped out just ahead of the horse.

'Whoa there,' I called out reassuringly. As though oblivious to my presence, the mare trotted on until she was almost level with me.

'Hike!' I shouted, translating into horse-driving terms. She pulled up instantly and looked at me enquiringly.

'What have you been up to?' I asked her as I quickly checked over her to see that she had suffered no ill-effects from her adventure. Totally unperplexed by the change of plan, the mare happily followed me back in the direction she had come from. It wasn't until then that I realised that she had travelled further than I thought and the halting site was by now a good half mile away. For a brief instant, thinking of the list of calls ahead of me, I was temped to hop up on her back and 'jockey' her home, but then thought better of it.

From a fair distance before reaching the entrance to the halting site, I was clearly visible to the Murphy family through the sparse blackberry bushes that offered a hedge around the site. Several faces appeared around the caravans and one by one the clan gathered to watch as we approached. The mare, as though sensing that the adventure was over, dragged her feet reluctantly, so that I was forced to encourage her repeatedly with a gentle flick of the rope. The silence from the gathering crowd was broken only by my intermittent 'Yup, mare' at my reluctant companion as I had long since given up trying to encourage her to 'Trot on.' From the apprehensive looks on the Travellers' faces, I glad that I was still on foot.

Having made my way up the broad driveway, lined on either side with an array of modern caravans, I headed straight for the person who was obviously the boss man.

'Good morning!' I called out in what I hoped was a friendly voice. As there was no immediate reply, I continued, 'I found this mare trotting up the road and thought she was probably one of yours.'

'Aye, that there's John-Joe's cob,' called out a young lad who looked no older than eight or nine. A frown from his mother silenced him.

'Ah that's fine, so,' I replied, beginning to feel unnerved by the silence. 'I'll leave her with you, then,' and I offered the frayed blue rope to a tall, but slightly wizened man, who had the look of being in charge. With a flick of his hand, he indicated another man, whom I assumed to be John-Joe.

'Take the mare,' he told him in a surprisingly deep voice, without taking his eyes off me.

As my companion was led off with a rally of 'Yup, mare' and 'Gowan up', the crowd gradually filtered away.

Feeling in some way that I had offended them, I turned away and headed back down the driveway, conscious of scurrying feet and giggling children behind me.

'Missis,' called the deep voice from behind me. I turned back, not knowing what to expect. 'Thank ye kindly, Missis. Thank ye,' and he turned away.

I had all but forgotten this brief incident when, a few weeks later, I got a call from the office just as I was heading off for lunch.

'Paddy Murphy from the halting site was just on. He said he has a foal with a bad cut and they want you to call out as soon as you can.'

'Me?' I questioned in surprise as, until now, Seamus had always dealt with the Murphys. 'But, sure, they don't even know me.'

'He was adamant they wanted you,' she repeated. 'He said something about you bringing back a horse of theirs.'

I was amazed because, at the time, I didn't think they knew who I was. The car had been parked some distance away and I had been wearing nothing more incriminating than an ordinary pair of jeans and the customary wax jacket.

Although my stomach was feeling a little hollow, I was curious and decided to go straight out to see what was wrong with the foal.

The same cluster of people was gathered, awaiting my arrival, this time on the small patch of grass at the back of the enclosure. My self-consciousness grew as the crowd parted to let my car by. I instantly recognised the same mare and beside her, a sturdy-looking foal. There was a subdued hum as I got out. But any awkwardness I felt vanished instantly the moment I saw the foal's hind-leg. Although from the front nothing seemed amiss, the whole hind-quarter was stained deep red with blood, some congealed and caked on the hairy coat, but still with a trickle of fresh blood oozing from the wound. This time I didn't notice the silence as I bent down beside the pretty filly foal to inspect the damage. The whole inner side of the leg was exposed as a vast skin flap hung uselessly away from the complex structures of muscles they had once covered. I followed the wound up to the top of the inner-leg and, right up where the leg met the belly, I could see that the foal had obviously become ensnared in some sort of wire. I guessed that it was barbed wire because of the macerated appearance of the deep, fleshy wound. A reasonable supply of blood was still oozing at a rate faster than I was comfortable with from a small foal.

'This is bad news,' I said softly to Paddy, who stood at my right-hand side.

'Ah Jaysus, Mary and Joseph,' implored one of the women from behind.

'Quiet, woman,' he growled and I jumped, thinking he was talking to me.

'Can ye fix it?' he asked, as though it were that simple.

'Maybe. Maybe not,' I replied, as much to myself as in answer. My mind was mentally running through the list of possible complications: blood loss, anaesthetic risk, tetanus, infection … I was down to contra-lateral laminitis when he interrupted me.

'If ye can fix it, do it,' he commanded.

'Well, it's not that simple,' I began. 'It would involve major work and a huge amount of aftercare. The whole job will end up costing more than the foal is worth and even with that, she might not make it. You might be better off putting her to sleep.'

I could see I wasn't convincing him, so I carried on, 'Even with the best of care, there's a high risk that she'll get an infection or even –'

'Listen te me now,' he interrupted in a low voice, bending in towards me. 'That there foal is worth more than money te me. If ye can fix it, then fix it.'

With that, he turned away from me, preventing me from expanding any further on the possible outcome or risks. I thought resignedly of the nice consent form that I would usually print out for a job like this, listing all the risks and possible complications, and sighed deeply, bitterly regretting the day I had found the mare on the road and earned the confidence of the Travellers.

With the combination of an extensive wound, a neonatal patient and a large crowd, I decided to return to the office for back-up. Having administered some intravenous antibiotics, a protective dose of anti-tetanus and some pain relief, I left with the promise to return as soon as possible.

'Are you busy?' I asked Seamus as I returned to the surgery with the benefit of a twenty-minute drive to plan my approach.

'Well, by the looks of it, I'm going to be,' he replied warily, eyeing the surgical and anaesthetic kits as I pulled them out of the back press.

'Which do you want to do?' I asked him, offering him either kit with a grin.

By the time we returned to the halting site, I had filled him in on the story.

He was doubtful. 'Nasty place to get a wound; too much movement to allow for good healing,' he said thoughtfully.

'Yes, and she's only about two weeks old, and it looks like it was barbed wire – probably good and rusty – and there isn't a stable or anything like it,' I continued cheerfully, now that I had back-up. 'But sure, they want to try and referral isn't an option, so what have we to lose?' I implored him.

'A lot of wasted time and money,' he retorted grimly.

Although by now I felt competent when anaesthetising small animals, a young foal was a different story. I was glad to hand over to Seamus and watched as he carefully drew from a vial of valium and mixed it with a minute amount of ketamine.

My request for hot water was silently fulfilled with a 'Right so,' as Paddy nodded almost imperceptibly at John-Joe.

'You ready to go?' enquired Seamus.

Within minutes, the little foal lay peacefully on the sparse grass that was to serve as the operating theatre.

Happy that Seamus was there to supervise the even, deep breathing of the patient and look after crowd control, I was soon engrossed in the ravaged remains of the hind-limb. Having filled the large wound with almost a full tube of gel, I carefully clipped away what remained of the fine coat, most of which was caked in clotted blood. Methodically, I washed away any obvious dirt and debris from the exposed area. Only then did I begin to examine the extent of the damage to the leg. The large flap of skin that been pulled down in ragged strips by the barbed wire was obviously long since devoid of blood supply. 'That'll have to go,' I muttered to myself, oblivious to the apprehension of my onlookers.

Carefully, I trimmed away the large skin flap, pleased to see oozing of fresh blood from the edge where I cut away. Once the skin was trimmed of any dead tissue, I inspected the lower layers. One of the main muscles was torn, almost completely, exposing the main blood supply to the hind-limb, which was, thankfully, still intact. As the wound was so fresh, it was only a matter of some careful suturing to restore the muscle to normality. In an older horse, I would have been much more concerned that the weight of a mature animal might be enough to break down my careful repair, but in a foal such as this one, which I estimated to weigh no more than sixty or seventy kilograms, I was somewhat optimistic. It would have been best to cast the leg to prevent excessive movement, but due to the position of the injury, that wasn't possible. At the very least, I would have liked to keep the foal confined, to limit the usual antics of an enthusiastic youngster. Looking around the bleak expanse of wasteland around the halting site, I knew this wasn't going to happen either.

With the muscle repaired, I turned my attention to the rest of the wound which by now was looking decidedly healthier.

'Would one of you mind holding up the fluid bag for me?' I enquired of my silent audience, nodding at the gallon of saline to which I had attached a giving set.

There was a lot of mumbling and shuffling before Paddy himself came forward. 'Just hold the bag up high and squeeze it as hard as you can to ensure an adequate flow,' I added. He was an efficient assistant as he wordlessly directed the flow of sterile fluid over the damaged tissue, while I swabbed and trimmed away any dirt or damaged tissue.

I prodded and probed with a forceps, carefully searching for any further damage. On a couple of occasions the forceps opened into a tiny dead end where a barb of wire had torn through the connective tissue surrounding the muscle body. At last I was satisfied that as much contamination as possible had been washed away.

Engrossed as I was in the fiddly task, it wasn't until I noticed the flow of saline slowing down that I looked back towards my assistant. Paddy, who looked to be a sturdy, well-built man, was red in the face with exertion as he struggled to hold the second gallon bag of saline up over his head.

'Paddy, would you mind giving Seamus a hand now because we're almost ready to let the foal come around. If you could stay at the head in case she tries to get up too quickly,' I asked him. 'You can give the bag to someone else,' I added, relieving him of his burden without embarrassing him too much.

Another person was silently pushed forward to continue the task.

My suturing was limited to areas where I could pull enough tissue together to make some attempt to reduce the size of the wound. Painstakingly, I inserted row after row of tiny sutures at several different angles, hoping to draw together the sub-cutaneous tissue and even some skin.

'Right, so. What do you think of that?' I asked Seamus, indicating the damaged limb.

'Well, it's as much as can be done, but it still has a long way to go,' he replied cautiously.

I arched my back slowly, until the dull ache receded before straightening myself up off my knees into a standing position.

'She won't be long now,' said Seamus, flicking at the corner of the foal's eyelid, watching as the enormous black eyelashes flickered in response, an indication that the anaesthetic was starting to wear off.

The usual banter that would accompany a moment like this was glaringly absent as my attempts to engage the

Travellers in light conversation failed miserably.

Covering the injury was impossible, but I applied a padded bandage to the lower limb to help prevent swelling from the inflammatory fluid which would inevitably build up below the wound. As an afterthought, I applied a similar bandage to the other hind limb to protect it from the extra weight it was going to have to bear for the duration of the recovery.

'Well, that's all we can do for the moment. Who's going to be in charge of her now?' I enquired, knowing that the aftercare for a wound like this was far more important than my own role.

John-Joe came forward with a miniature version of himself a step behind. 'Well, it's John-Joe Junior's foal, so I suppose we'll be looking after her.'

'Wow! A foal of your own,' I replied in surprise to the young lad, half hidden behind his father's coat.

'Got it for me Confirmation,' came the reply. He was obviously bursting with pride as his chest puffed up and he took a step forward.

'Well, we'll have to take extra good care of her, so. I would really like to confine her in a small paddock,' I began, thinking of the carefully sutured muscle, 'but on the other hand, walking around will help to keep the swelling down. Will she lead for you?' I asked the young lad as he was by now brave enough to meet my eye.

'Oh be God and she will, Miss, if I folly 'er on behind the mare,' he confirmed, a determined look in his eye.

'Well, the more you lead her around the better she'll be,' I told him.

By the time I had finished going through the daily wound care, the foal was up, wobbling precariously as she tried to readjust herself. I was pleased to see that the offending limb was touching the ground with each faltering step.

I had cleared the site of my temporary theatre and was packing up to go when I heard Seamus saying to John-Joe, 'We'll be needing a few bob, so.'

Paddy was quick to reply. 'Give the man there his money.'

A figure was negotiated and a wad of twenty-euro notes, the thickness of a telephone directory, was pulled out.

'I always knew we were in the wrong job,' said Seamus to me as soon as I joined him in the car, having promised to call back in the morning.

The next morning saw one of many calls that I made to the Murphys over the following weeks. Luckily, their road was one we passed frequently on our daily calls, so after a few days, I took to dropping in whenever I was in the area instead of sticking to pre-booked times. John-Joe junior, or JJ, as I soon found out he was called, became my permanent shadow, mysteriously showing up every time I arrived. Although I was always followed, at a distance, by a straggle of his young comrades, it was only ever JJ who spoke to me. For the first week, the wound continuously discharged a sticky yellow fluid as the body derided itself of remaining unhealthy tissue.

'I don't like the look of that there stuff, Missis,' JJ would comment, nodding his head wisely.

'Don't be worrying about it,' I would tell him and try to explain how the body was getting rid of all the bad bits. 'As soon as all the bad stuff is gone, the wound will start to heal,' I assured him, seeing the constant doubt in his eyes.

'Smell it,' I told him. 'There's no poison in the blood there,' I continued, well aware of the Travellers' aversion to the all-encompassing malady of 'poison in the blood'.

I showed him how to clean the wound, supervising the boiling of the kettle in the cluttered, yet tidy caravan into which I was hesitantly invited.

'Stick your hand in there now,' I invited him so that he would know the correct water temperature as the clean bucket of water cooled.

The foal became accustomed to the repeated washing of the leg, as she stood obediently, tied to a tap at a discarded bath in the yard. JJ was a diligent student and became quite meticulous, waiting for the crusted discharge to soften before gently wiping it away. Before each cleaning, the hairless skin below the wound would be copiously covered with petroleum jelly to prevent scalding of the baby-soft tissue.

When JJ had become proficient at cleaning the wound, I showed him how to change the supportive bandage on the leg, which he carried on doing at regular intervals.

After the first week, I began to call less often as the wound had stopped discharging and was now, ever so slowly, beginning to heal. With each visit, I carefully studied the outlines of the wound and could see the pale, thin, hairless margin gradually beginning to close in over the large triangle of what looked like healthy granulation tissue. With the combination of JJ's administrations, the healing powers of a young animal and the merciful absence of flies, we were beginning to win the battle.

'What d'ye think of 'er now, Missis?' became the opening question every time I called.

Although I continued to remind JJ that complications could still arise, I myself was becoming quietly optimistic. With the skill of generations of folklore, Paddy confidently assured me that the warm weather would not come until late that season. I hoped he was right as it would give us the two months that I estimated it would take the wound to heal completely. Once the warm weather came, we would be plagued by the intrusion of flies who would gorge themselves on the feast of flesh and lay innocent-looking eggs which would hatch into maggots and burrow into the tender flesh, effectively putting an end to all our good work.

By now, I reckoned that JJ had all the skills he needed to carry on with the foal with only occasional supervision. I noticed that the vet wraps had been changed to strips of cloth, which, although far from the ideal bandaging material, were always clean and carefully applied when I checked them.

Often I drove by to see JJ, or very rarely one of the other lads, leading the foal around the field in lackadaisical, haphazard patterns as though they had spent the afternoon at the task. Only the slightest lameness gave any indication of her wound. Despite the severity of the injury, the foal continued to grow and thrive.

I had almost stopped worrying about my patient when I

got a call late one afternoon. One of the local welfare groups had received a complaint from a concerned member of the public about an ill-treated, injured foal.

'The foal is out there in the halting site, the one up past the factory,' said Kevin, the inspector on duty.

Although most of the staff were genuine, well-intentioned people, Kevin was new to the group and seemed be trying too hard to prove himself – and to the wrong people. In my limited experience of him, I found him to be more interested in the accent of the owner than the condition of the animal under investigation, and his knowledge of animal matters often left much to be desired.

'You mean Murphys' place?' I questioned, as in all my visits I hadn't come across any other foal, though I didn't for a minute associate the complaint with 'the filly' as she was always called.

'Yes. I think that's the place,' replied Kevin. 'Apparently there is a very badly injured piebald foal being dragged around the field all day by some kids. This lady said that they are at it every time she passes.'

'A piebald filly foal?' I questioned, despairing yet again at the ignorance that sometimes makes supposed do-gooders rush to the aid of an animal that was managing perfectly well without them. 'If it's the one I'm thinking about, it's one that got badly cut as a young foal,' I told Kevin, 'but I've been treating her for the past two months. The young lad that owns her is an absolute cracker. All that "dragging her around the field" has probably saved her life.'

'But this lady,' continued Kevin, sounding slightly disappointed that the drama might be plucked from his hands, 'was adamant that the animal in question is lame and needs to be taken away for proper care.'

'Of course the foal is lame,' I replied wearily. 'So would the "lady" be if she had a deep, open wound on her leg. Listen, Kevin, those young lads are playing a blinder with that foal. Seamus and I were fairly cagey about treating her in the first place, she was so badly injured. With all the work the young lad has put into her, she is doing way better than I thought. The way she's going, she's going to make a complete recovery.'

'Well, I suppose if you're sure, we'll let it go for the moment, but I'll just pay a visit out to them to keep an eye on them anyway.'

'Kevin,' I replied in even, measured tones, 'that foal is under my care and is being looked after one hundred percent. You don't need to call out to her.'

'Well, we'll keep an eye on them, anyway. The lady who reported them was adamant that the foal was in distress. She has a very big yard on the far side of the hill.'

I tried to get back out to the halting-site that evening, but the never-ending backlog of spring kept me away that day and the next. I wasn't worried as I knew all was going well. It was just reaching twilight when I pulled in on the Friday evening. I was surprised that JJ didn't join me on the driveway and the sketchy silhouette of the various families outlined by the light of the camp fire stayed put.

My usual greeting was left unanswered and JJ stood, eyes cast down to the ground. 'What's up, JJ? Is the filly okay?' I called out to him, as a knot grew in my stomach. If we were going to have a problem with the wound, I had thought it would have happened before now.

I was surprised at the aggression in Paddy's tone as he spat out at me. 'You tell us how she is. Your friend that took her away should know.'

'My friend? That took her away?' I replied in genuine bewilderment.

'Came with a box yesterday and told us he was taking her away to be looked after.'

'He took the foal way!' I repeated stupidly, conscious of the deep well of anger building up inside me. 'Who took her away? What friend of mine?' I demanded, noticing out of the side of my eye that young JJ was standing, fists clenched by his side, tears streaming down his face.

'That Kevin what's-his-name. Said he'd been talking te ye,' shouted Paddy, not noticing my reaction.

'Listen here, Paddy,' I replied. 'Kevin, whatever-his-name-is is no friend of mine and yes, he did talk to me and I told him the filly was being well looked after and that there was no need for him to get involved.'

The silence that followed as Paddy, JJ and the rest of the clan struggled to believe me was broken only by the crackling and sparks of an old section of dried-out wood on the fire that seemed to match the tension between us.

'Why' I continued after a few moments 'would I get them to take the foal away now? If I'd had any worries wouldn't I have got them to take her six weeks ago?'

The impasse was broken as JJ crossed over from behind the fire to where I stood.

'They couldn't even load her right, Missis,' he informed me. 'Made a right bollix of it they did, fussing at 'er and shoving 'er when all she needed was to let her folly in behind the mare. Let out a right kick at yer man, she did,' he carried on, obviously proud of his charge.

'Go on with ye,' growled Paddy at JJ, but without the usual gruffness of tone.

Despite the tension, I had to quell the bubble of laughter that rose within me at the thought of the little filly giving as good as she got.

'Paddy, leave it with me. I'll sort it out, I promise you,' I assured him.

He stared at me in the bright glow of the fire. 'I'll believe ye, boss. Ye'r always as good as yer word,' he declared.

As I turned away I hid a smile at the promotion in the eyes of the Travellers to being the 'boss'.

The next morning, I headed up to the office where Kevin worked before going to the surgery. What Seamus didn't know about wasn't going to worry him, I thought to myself, at least not until it was all over anyway.

Kevin was skulking in behind the reception area when I arrived and quickly tried to make his way out the back door when he saw me coming.

'Where is she?' I demanded.

'She? Who's she? I don't know what you're talking about.'

'You know well who I'm talking about. Where's the piebald filly?'

'Oh her,' he replied airily. 'You needn't worry about her. We have had one of our other vets out to have a look at her already. She's in good hands.'

'Kevin,' I said, through clenched teeth, taking one, two, and a few more deep breaths before continuing, 'I am treating that foal. After this evening's surgery, I'm going out to the halting-site to check on her, like I do a few days a week and have done for the past six weeks. You just make sure she's there,' I finished, not bothering to wait for his reply.

On the way back to the office, I made a few calls to the other local vets. The first two knew nothing about it and I left a message for the third, who rang me back an hour later.

'A little piebald foal,' he confirmed when I asked if he was treating any animals for the welfare group. 'I went up to one there yesterday, all right. Bad old wound on the hind leg, but it seemed to be doing nicely to me.'

He commiserated when I told him the story. 'Listen, whatever you want to do just let me know and I'll back you on it. Whoever is looking after her is doing a good job.'

There was no need to ring him back. That evening, I pulled in to the halting-site again. From the entrance, the scene was the same – the outline of silhouettes in the bright glow of the campfire, but this time, a small figure came running out to meet me.

'She's back, boss! She's back!' he roared at me from half-way down the drive.

The filly foal never looked back. Before the first of the flies started, the wound had fully closed over. I didn't see her after that for a long time until one autumn evening when I called by to look at one of the other horses. The little filly was, by then, quite a substantial filly and as I made my way over to her, she turned her hind-quarters to me and lashed out in high-spiritedness before taking off at a gallop, without the slightest trace of a limp.

CHAPTER THIRTEEN

A CASE OF BUMBLE FOOT

'**B**ase to bald eagle,' came the familiar tones over the phone. 'Bald eagle to base,' I replied automatically. 'What's the crack, Sean?'

'I have another one for you,' he replied.

'Another buzzard … or a real bald eagle?' I enquired, suspending my disbelief.

'No. Nothing as fancy as that,' he laughed. 'It's a turkey cock.'

'A turkey cock! What do you want to do with a turkey cock? How about a barbecue?' I asked. 'I could manage that all right.'

'This is a serious stud turkey that a mate of mine owns. Problem is, he's gone lame – looks like a case of bumble foot to me.'

'Bumble foot?' repeated Donal incredulously when I

told him that night. 'He's having you on. What the hell is bumble foot?'

'It's an infection in the foot. Apparently his friend is very knowledgeable about his poultry and has been treating it for weeks, but it's getting worse. He needs surgery.'

'So you're going to operate on a lame turkey cock?' Donal stated. 'With bumble foot! What does Seamus think of that?'

When I told him the next morning, Seamus was equally unimpressed. 'What did you plan on charging for it?' he asked, already having a fair idea.

'Well, it's a turkey. I can't really go to town on him.'

'Oh, great! Is he a cousin of the buzzard? Are they going to give us a load of repeat business or bring in new clients or something?'

'Well, I'll do it in my own time, so you won't even see it here. Unless, of course, you'd like to do the anaesthetic …' I trailed off, noting the lack of enthusiasm in his face.

So, Sunday morning saw just myself, Sean and Roger the turkey cock preparing for my maiden venture into turkey surgery. Molly's biggest plastic toy box served as a 'knock-down' box into which I had drilled a hole for the anaesthetic tube to be placed. Roger wasn't overly impressed as we bundled him in, but soon his broad neck flopped to one side as the anaesthetic overcame him. Before he knew it, he was plucked and prepped on the surgery table and I have to admit that he did look slightly incongruous, draped in surgical green instead the usual oven bag. However, it was no laughing matter when I turned my attention to the infected foot which had led him here. Although

Sean's friend was a dedicated bird man and had methodically cleaned the foot and dosed him with antibiotics, the necrotic, angry-looking tissue seemed to have won out. As I cut through the worst of it, I noticed that my scalpel blade induced no haemorrhage, indicating that the tissue was dead. I trimmed away the devitalised flesh further and further and couldn't help thinking of the old advice: 'First, do no harm' that had been drilled into us.

'I don't know if this is going anywhere,' I said to Sean as I trimmed away still more tissue.

'Ah, that's what you said about the bald eagle and look at him,' he replied. 'Go on! He'll be grand,' he assured me with the confidence of one who wasn't holding the knife.

'Well, if he can't get around when he wakes up, I'm putting him down,' I said as much to myself as to Sean, knowing that the owner had already signed the appropriate consent form.

Eventually, I came to oozing blood, although the tissue still looked very angry. Having flushed the whole area with two litres of heated saline, I packed it carefully with the antibiotic beads I had prepared that morning. Finally, I sutured together what remained of the web as best I could.

When he came around, Roger gobbled away to himself, and to my surprise didn't seem too put out by the whole affair. I made a note to myself to add to the growing anecdotal evidence list in relation to the use of the anaesthetic and anti-inflammatory medications in turkey cocks.

I laughed to myself as I filled out the discharge instructions and it took every ounce of my self-control not to write 'twenty minutes to the pound' on his aftercare sheet.

Despite my misgivings, Roger, after numerous repeat visits to dress the wound, eventually returned to his former glory and bore his scars proudly without any obvious signs of pain or lameness. Seamus wasn't overly impressed when we eventually did get payment in the form of an oven-ready offspring the following Christmas.

Sadly, it seemed that that was to be the zenith of my avian career. From then on things went downhill.

By coincidence, we went through a phase of getting a lot of bird clients in the Blue Cross. I assumed this was less to do with my brilliance as a turkey surgeon some forty-odd miles away and more to do with the fact that no-one else in north Dublin was interested in treating them! Although the Blue Cross was, by its nature, limited in many respects, we generally managed to do what was needed for the multitude of dogs, cats and other furries that came our way. Feathered patients, however, are a lot more susceptible to stress, which meant that the Blue Cross mobile clinic wasn't really ideal.

In an attempt to limit death from the sheer stress of queuing on the side of a roundabout alongside an array of natural predators, we included a 'birds first' policy in our general triage system. Despite the protest from the rest of the queue, Eamon took to ushering the birds first into the dubious safety of the clinic where we could get them treated, and hopefully home, before they died of shock.

One Wednesday evening, having muddled my way through a couple of canaries with mites, a budgie with an overgrown beak and a magpie fledgling that had fallen out of a nest, Eamon gave a shout through the door, 'One more for you out here!' A collection of assorted mutts and moggies had piled up inside the tiny waiting room at the end of the van so we opened the other door to allow the last bird through. Out of a poky cage, covered in a child's furry blanket, came a spectacular-looking African Grey Parrot.

'It's only 'is travelling cage,' the owner assured me.

'What's up with him?' I asked. 'He looks the picture of health to me.'

'Ah, sure, he's in great form, so 'e is. It's just dat 'is nails need clippin'.'

'That's no problem,' I assured him, relieved that it was nothing too demanding or complicated for such a valuable bird. As I hunted in the drawer for the nail clippers, I told him, 'You know, you really should bring a bird like this to a private vet – this clinic is for welfare cases only and we're not really set up for birds.' I knew that the cost of the bird could well have paid for the entire clinic for at least a month. Ideally, I would have sent him away, but then the parrot would have had to go through the stress of yet another veterinary visit. 'I'll clip his nails for you this time, as he is here now, but in future a private clinic would be better if you can afford it.'

'Nah! Hector won't mind dis,' he said, indicating the crowd outside with a jerk of his head. 'Anyway, I did bring 'im to some posh place out dere in de village bu' dey told me not te bring 'im back no more.'

'Oh, is that right?' I questioned, wondering what I had let myself in for. Parrots are notorious for biting, although this guy did seem to be well handled. 'And why was that?'

'Dunno,' he replied and let the matter drop.

Reluctantly, I picked up the clippers and took a firm hold of the claw while Hector waited, innocently perched on his owner's arm. It was only when I raised the clippers towards him that he emitted a high-pitched shriek like a child in mortal danger. As I jumped, I dropped his leg and at that moment, he took off and sailed over my head, landing with a crash on the ledge containing our supply of tablets and injectables. Immediately he took off again, this time landing on the bandages which he promptly began to pick up with his beak and hurl with ferocity at the far wall. All the time, the child-like shriek continued. I could hear a mutter of discontent emerging from the waiting room – I was sure they were wondering who, or what, was being murdered. When the racket continued for a few more minutes, some brave soul decided to see what was going on. I watched in horror as Hector caught sight of the door being opened – and his route to freedom. In a flash, while Hector's attention was nailed to his escape route, Eamon managed to throw a large towel over him, just before the man opening the door slammed it in his face, obviously not brave enough to face an enraged parrot.

I thought that with our patient trapped we'd be able to do the job and get him home to relative safety, but as soon as I began to clip the nails, he started to hurl a rally of abuse at me with a selection of language that considerably broadened my English vocabulary. The faster I clipped, the more and the louder he shrieked at me, while his owner got increasingly red-faced.

'I got 'im offa me mate,' he assured me. 'I wudn't 'ave learned him dat!'

By the time the ordeal was over, the roars of verbal abuse of the parrot were almost drowned out by the convulsions of laughter erupting from the crowded waiting room next door. I was sweating by the time he left and oblivious to the sense of mirth and gaiety around the clinic. All I could see was the queue stretching almost as far as the roundabout.

With a sigh, I braced myself to open the door to the now rowdy waiting room as I let out a faint-hearted, 'Next, please.'

The next few weeks were mercifully bird-free, but one particularly wet and windy night we were half-way through the clinic when someone started beating down the doors. At first we ignored it, assuming that whoever it was would take their place in the queue. As the racket continued, however, Gordon glanced out the window and quickly turned back to me saying, 'You might want to let these ones in.' I assumed Gordon had good reason and readily agreed. A young couple, no more than twenty years old or so, stood before me holding a canary. Much and all as I worried about birds getting stressed at the clinic, this one was to set new standards. Although our avians usually arrived in a wide spectrum of pet-carriers, ranging from posh cages to old shoe boxes, this unfortunate canary came securely enclosed in no more than the hand of its loving owner.

I quickly subdued my outrage as I realised that the longer we delayed, the less the unfortunate canary's chances were. I didn't even bother to comment, but noticed Eamon rummaging among the presses for a box.

It got worse. The young owners launched into a detailed description of the bird's history. Bewildered as I was at their ignorance, it took a few moments for me to realise that the canary was, far from being in prime health, in fact, dead! As the girl waved her arms around, vividly gesticulating while she told their story, the tiny yellow head flopped feebly from side to side. I glanced over at Eamon and Gordon to find that the only ones who hadn't noticed were the owners. It was then that I saw the slightly glazed eyes and intense concentration of both the girl and her partner. I had to break her off, mid-flight, to explain that far from being fit and well, the bird was actually dead. It took a few moments for the stark reality to dawn and then, pausing as though to gather breath, she wailed at me: 'Ye'v killed me bleedin' bird. Some bloody vet you are. Der wasn't a bother on 'im till you gotta hold of 'im.'

At that point I had had enough and told her in no uncertain terms that I had never had a hold of him and that it was the hold *she* had on him that had killed him. A flash of argument followed during which neither myself nor Gordon nor Eamon could convince her of anything other than I had killed her bird. She stomped out of the clinic, still clutching the lifeless form and shouted out at the expectant crowd, 'Yez might as well go home. Dat bleedin' eejit of a vet just killed me bird.'

That seemed to put a halt to my bird cases for a while as I was then deemed to be 'bleedin' useless' with birds, but, strangely, the one group of bird people who until then had stayed away, suddenly began to appear. The pigeon fanciers started to come, although I regularly assured them that

I really knew little to nothing about pigeons. Most of them I managed to dispatch on the basis that our limited range of drugs did not include many pigeon products, but one guy got cute. He had already been to his local pet shop, where the owner had given him a non-prescription, oral supplement to dose his birds. The problem was, he assured me, that the pigeons didn't like the taste of it and would I mind dosing them for him? I was inclined to refuse, but when he offered what I thought was a considerable donation for the clinic, I reluctantly agreed. In he arrived with a wicker basket containing some forty pigeons of varying colours. 'Which one,' I asked him, 'is to be dosed?'

'The whole bleedin' lota dem, luv,' came his reply as he thrust the first one towards me.

I decided it would be quicker to do it than argue with him, but ten minutes later I was beginning to wonder as one after another the pigeons gagged and gasped as I dosed them. Finally, I got to the last one and stopped to do a quick tidy-up of feathers and pigeon droppings when the door opened and in he arrived with another basketful.

It was only when I was half-way through the third batch that I noticed a bit of a commotion going on outside. The usual flow of traffic seemed to be interrupted and the crowd outside, although usually boisterous, seemed to be in uniquely high spirits. I glanced out and noticed a pigeon fly by and then another, and then another.

I took one look at my wayward client, who stared back at me with open arms and said, 'Well, they are homin' birds, luv. Sure, they'll make their own way home. I promised te meet a mate in de pub before nine o'clock.'

When the clinic finally ended almost an hour late, the homing pigeons, whether confused by the local geography or still stunned by the dose they had got, were no further towards their intended destination. As I packed the car, a flock of pigeons circled around me and both Eamon and Gordon fell about the place laughing at my face as a variety of fantails, white tips and piebalds perched on the car and deposited their droppings around me.

'Would you look, Eamon,' said Gordon. 'Doesn't she look just like St Francis of Assisi there?'

'She does, all right,' agreed Eamon, ignoring my murderous looks. 'I suppose you could call her the vet among the pigeons!'

CHAPTER FOURTEEN

A NASTY FRACTURE

After my disastrous first effort at continued practice development courses in the equine world, I had resigned myself to the fact that I just really wasn't the academic type. A few courses of interest came and went, but I didn't avail of any of them. I carried on to the best of my ability, learning only from my own experience, with an inevitable amount of trial and error.

As time went on, though, I became increasingly aware of my limitations. For all the things I could now do with a little bit of competence, there were a hundred and one others that were still beyond my grasp.

Some days it bothered me. Others, it didn't. At the Blue Cross clinic in Ballyfermot one night, one of the regulars berated me as I prescribed a course of steroid tablets for her cat that was suffering from a neurological disorder. It was, by a coincidence, the same medication I had prescribed three months previously for a skin condition in her little Westie, and likely to be equally effective.

'Is that all yiz can do for me?' she questioned, looking disdainfully at the medication envelope. 'I was watchin' de vets on de TV the udder evening. Doin' cat scans and tings like dat, dey were. Bleedin' real vets dey have over der, not like yous lot,' she ended, casting a disparaging look over the crew. With that she stomped out of the clinic, carelessly throwing a two-euro coin in the box as she went – the sum total of her donation towards the treatment.

While working in Ballyfermot, I was more than happy to refer clients to the referral practices that worked with the Blue Cross, as only basic medical treatments were carried out at the clinic. But back at the practice in Wicklow, referrals seemed to me to epitomise failure. At the time, it didn't occur to me that recognising your limitations and knowing when and where to send a patient was a skill in itself.

My main interest was in surgery and I had already studied, in some depth, the various techniques for a wide range of surgical procedures and, more specifically, orthopaedic procedures. With some knowledge, but very little practical experience, I itched to get my hands on each new fracture that presented, and became increasingly frustrated when I would have to refer a case to the veterinary college or, worse still, simply amputate the limb as the owner could not, or would not, pay for the cost of a referral to a specialist hospital.

When the brochure for an orthopaedic course, consisting of five weekends over a two-year period, arrived in the office, I booked immediately, despite my misgivings. As I went on my daily calls, every three-legged dog I passed on the road seemed to mock me, regardless of whether I or one of my predecessors had been responsible.

The course itself, although exhausting, was a revelation. The first Friday evening began with each delegate having to introduce themselves to the group and recount the story of their worst orthopaedic disaster. To my embarrassment, I had nothing to say as I had never carried out any orthopaedic procedures other than a few salvage amputations! Nonetheless, the mood was set for the course as we all knew each other's worst. Intensive lectures followed, alternating between two surgeons, both of whom, unlike their equine counterparts, skimmed quickly over their own impressive qualifications before carrying on with the lectures. Despite their obviously vast experience, neither seemed to take himself too seriously and spent a lot of time showing cases that had gone wrong, allowing us to learn by their experiences so we wouldn't have to learn from our own mistakes. Although intensive, the sessions were well lightened by the slagging and banter that took place between both lecturers and delegates. Unlike my previous experience, all the information was very specific and totally geared towards enabling you to do the job when back in practice.

I drove home after the first session on a high of depth gauges and drill bits, screw diameters and sizes. The Saturday morning continued with lectures which led to an afternoon of 'cadaver practicals' – putting the lectures into practice on real, although sadly, deceased, canine bodies. By Saturday afternoon, I was delighted to find myself happily drilling a pin into a femur and wiring it in place with a series of orthopaedic wires.

The twenty delegates were a very mixed group, some totally green, like myself, but also including people who could probably have given the course themselves, but all with an interest in orthopaedics. The whole atmosphere was one of total enthusiasm, with the more experienced vets delighted to show 'the youngsters', like myself, their own little tips and techniques. The lunchtimes and tea-breaks ended up being just as informative as the practical sessions and lectures. By the first Sunday afternoon, I came away with one job offer – should I ever want to take it – and a few phone numbers of like-minded vets with whom I still keep in touch.

As usual, Seamus wasn't overly enthusiastic with my new-found skills. He laughed when I displayed the new 'toys' that I had ordered while on the course – the basic tools to carry out some orthopaedic repairs. While I waited for a suitable case, it was noticeable that the queues in the evening clinics lengthened considerably as each patient was treated to a thorough orthopaedic examination, regardless of their presenting problem.

With the second part of the course not due until the following spring, my enthusiasm had waned somewhat by Christmas, when I still hadn't had a chance to put any of my new skills to use. It seemed that the cats and dogs of Wicklow had developed an innate street sense that they had previously lacked. The lectures themselves were gradually becoming a bit of a blur.

However, one morning in January, a time of year when mixed practice is usually relatively quiet, Arthur rang to tell me that he had admitted a dog he thought might need to have his leg pinned. I was ecstatic, hoping against all hope that the fracture would be a type that had been covered in the first course. Skipping lunch, I rushed back to the practice to find a handsome German Shepherd sitting expectantly in the kennels. His radiographs were on the viewing box and as I stared at the clear images on the screen, I tried to convince myself that this was the perfect case. The fractured bone in question was a femur, the long bone running from the hip to the knee. The fracture itself was oblique, spiraling from the top end to half way down the shaft. I tried to ignore a few jagged fragments and the sheer size of the bone and the weight of the dog himself.

A very first session of the now distant orthopaedic course had been spent discussing fracture scoring. This involved a thorough assessment of each particular fracture and how it might have happened, the nature of not only the patient in question, but also the owner. Carefully, I assessed the dog himself, his giant weight and athletic potential, the type of fracture, the fragments, and reluctantly acknowledged that a pin and wire repair wasn't going to be the best option. The sheer size and activity of the dog and the obvious velocity of the impact that had created the fracture all pushed me towards a bone plate, although, sadly, I realised that bone plating would not be covered until the following course! Having carefully weighed up all the options, I picked up the phone to ring the owner. Mrs Devlin sounded very hesitant as I outlined my plans. Ideally, I explained, Boris would be sent to the veterinary college for a bone plate, but when I gave a rough estimate of cost, the sharp intake of breath suggested that this was not going to happen. I continued to outline the option of a pin and wire, trying to emphasise that the repair would not be as stable as the first option and therefore, would be less likely to succeed. I gave what I thought was a fair quote, significantly cheaper than the first option, but Mrs Devlin didn't sound a whole lot more enthusiastic. The only other option, I informed her, would be to have the dog put to sleep; amputating a hind leg in a large, active German Shepherd would be a disaster.

'I'll have a chat with Jimmy and get back to you,' she told me quickly. 'Although,' she continued, 'he does have a brother who is good with the auld hounds. We might give him a ring and see if he could do anything. His father had a dog once with a broken leg that healed up right well without any of them fancy things you're talking about.'

I looked in despair from my shiny new tool box to the unfortunate Boris and wondered why I had bothered. 'They just don't get it, do they?' I complained to Boris. He whimpered slightly as he shifted his weight onto his good limb and then lay down, head dejectedly between his broad paws.

It seemed that 'the brother' was losing his touch some-what as no mention was made of him when Mrs Devlin's other half arrived at the surgery later that day.

With only a passing glance at Boris, he wrung his hands, and leaning his massive weight against the consulting table said that they had decided the best option would be to put the dog to sleep. Although I wasn't altogether surprised, I couldn't believe that Boris wasn't even going to be given a chance. What, I thought to myself, was the

point in going to courses and investing heavily in special-
ised surgical equipment when people didn't want the
treatment for their animals?

'Well, I told you that, didn't I?' said Seamus as I relayed
my tale of woe to him the next morning. 'You were the
one running off to do your course.'

A regular part of veterinary practice involves euthanasia
of animals: some much-loved pets at the end of a long road,
others following serious illness or injury but, sadly, too
many for the simple reason that they are unwanted. Boris
fell in between two categories, but it sickened me to think
of such a magnificent animal not being given a chance.

Not long after Mr Devlin had left the surgery, I dialled
the house number. Mrs Devlin sounded surprised to hear
from me.

'Oh, it's yourself, is it?' she said. 'Ah the poor old dog,
isn't it a terrible pity? But there was nothing to be done for
the brute,' she added as though in defiance of my lengthy
lecture earlier that day.

'Well, the thing is, Mrs Devlin, I was wondering, as you
want to have Boris put to sleep, would you mind if we
were to take over his ownership? I will do the surgery
myself at my own expense and re-home him afterwards if
his leg heals.'

As I spoke to her, I tried to ignore not only Seamus's reaction at what was probably quite an unprofessional sugges-
tion and also Donal's when he realised that we would be
inheriting yet another dog for the recovery period and one
that was going to involve a lot of time and aftercare.

Mrs Devlin didn't take too much persuading. I realised

just how genuine she was in her declared affection for the dog when she magnanimously offered to take him back when he had made a full recovery, if all went well. 'But only,' she reiterated, 'if he doesn't have a limp or anything like that.' She seemed unfazed when I told her she would have to legally sign the dog over to me.

Donal was delighted for me that at last I had succeeded in obtaining a real orthopaedic case, but not as enthusiastic when he realised that Boris would be coming to stay with us for a while after the surgery. Although, ideally, I would like to have kept Boris until he was fully recovered and ready for rehoming, the imminent arrival of Molly's sibling meant that I would have to organise for one of the local welfare groups to take over his care a few weeks after the surgery.

For the next few days, while I ordered the correct size pins and wire, Boris stayed at the surgery where daily treatment helped to reduce the tissue swelling in preparation for his surgery.

The night before the surgery I slept amongst an array of surgical atlases, course notes and any other relevant articles I could get my hands on. The surgical kit was duly sterilised and the battery for the drill fully charged.

On the fateful morning, Boris lazily wagged his tail as I slowly injected the intravenous anaesthetic. He was, by now, quite fond of me.

Arthur had readily agreed to assist at the surgery. He was happy to observe the procedure without the responsibility of actually doing it, and I was glad to have a bit of 'professional hand-holding', even though he had never done any orthopaedic work himself. With Boris sleeping peacefully, I suspended the entire hind leg from a hook in the ceiling and carefully clipped the leg until it resembled an over-sized, if somewhat bruised, chicken drumstick. I wrapped the paw in a sterile drape before draping the surgical site. Once Boris was prepared, I scrubbed and gowned, finally putting on the sterile gloves before taking a last look at the surgical atlas, reminding me somewhat of a recipe book, propped up on the shelf behind.

It was only as I started to prepare for my incision that I really noticed the amount of swelling and discolouration in the area over the shaft of the femur. My surgical atlas displayed, in simple line diagrams, the site of the incision which would expose the two main muscle bodies. The next page indicated the shaft of the femur which would lie directly underneath, once I had separated the muscle mass. Tentatively, I prodded the area, hesitating for a few moments, trying to decide where exactly to make the incision in the distorted limb. Finally, taking a few deep breaths, I sliced an incision over a ten-centimetre-long section of the leg. Dark, red, watery fluid oozed out along the full length. Arthur diligently swabbed the site with sterile gauze so that I would have a clear view of what lay beneath.

I glanced back at the picture in my atlas, feeling slightly disconcerted that it wasn't looking terribly similar. Cautiously, I started to separate the edges of the skin and pick at bits of traumatised connective tissue or fasciae. I suddenly noticed I was feeling rather hot, although it was cold in the operating room in mid-winter and my knees had taken on a rather jelly-like consistency that had nothing to do with my state of advanced pregnancy.

After some time, during which I cautiously stabbed at the oedematous fasciae, I noticed Arthur glancing at his watch.

'So, what's next?' he eventually asked.

'Well, I just have to find the divide between the two muscles, but,' I added, glancing again at the simple line drawing, 'the cadavers we operated on in the course didn't have a half a pound of mince meat in there.'

I couldn't understand why he laughed as, by now, a cold gush of fear was starting to seep through me.

Eventually, I could swab no more and had to try to discern the muscle divide. A few times I picked up the tissue forceps and Metzenbaum scissors and half-heartedly incised in what I thought was the right area. The glistening strip of fasciae that should have acted as my guideline had long since disappeared, lost in a mass of traumatised tissue.

Eventually, the tips of the scissors divided the two muscles, although I suspected not exactly at the right place. At an agonising pace, I swabbed and fiddled and eventually opened the divide to match the length of my initial incision, although the distal end did run off at an angle over the last few centimetres or so. Finally, I put the instruments back in the tray and ran my finger deep into the incision until I was able to feel the bony shaft of the femur. With more force than I thought would have been necessary, I was eventually able to break down the tissue attached to the shaft, enough to feel my way to the roughened fracture end. Using a combination of gloved fingers, scissors tips and a periosteal elevator, I was, with difficulty, able to expose the point of the fracture at the proximal end, although it obstinately remained deep within the massive limb.

Arthur was, by now, looking like he regretted ever offering to help as I ignored any attempts at conversation, so intent was I on trying to figure out how I was ever going to complete the surgery.

In the time between completing the first surgical course and meeting Boris, I had read and reread the lecture notes. I had imprinted on my brain the importance of not traumatising the tissue and trying not to strip the muscle from the bone, as the muscle provided the blood supply that was essential for the repair of the fracture. That morning, I had vowed to leave every bit of muscle attached but, by now, my standards had dropped; I was now merely trying to expose the bone any way possible.

Having finally exposed the proximal end as best I could, I drew a few deep breaths and carefully tried to unravel my back and hunched shoulders before turning my attention to the other end of the fracture. All the time I had worked on freeing the jagged proximal end, I had been aware of the shaft of the femur running alongside. Now I ran my finger along its length, gradually breaking down the soft tissue attachments, and realised, with dismay, that the two ends of the bone overlapped by what seemed to be at least three centimetres.

I glanced up at the X-ray viewer to see the first radiograph which indicated an overlap of maybe half a centimetre. In the days in between, the strong musculature of the huge dog had contracted to an extent that the two ends looked like they would never meet again.

After my initial setback in trying to locate the femur, I had finally achieved it and quietly reassured myself that the hardest party was over. Now, with a sense of dread, it dawned on me that my work was only beginning.

Arthur, too, seemed to have noticed my dilemma and had stopped the smalltalk. 'How are you going to get the two ends together?' he asked quietly, annoying me with his assumption that I would know.

The surgery in the course had involved dead dogs, with artificial fractures that were in place and ready to repair. Little mention had been made of how to reduce the fracture or to realign the two ends of the bone. The surgical atlas neatly skipped from locating the fracture to sewing up the muscle layers afterwards.

It was only later that I realised with shock that it took almost an hour as I pulled and rotated and tried against all odds to get the two ends of the bone together. Arthur, similarly scrubbed up, followed my directions as he manipulated the end of the leg. With neither of us having any experience of what we were doing, it was agonisingly slow, as millimetre by millimetre we gradually made progress.

In all the time, I drew consolation from the fact that Boris's anaesthetic was the only part of the case that could be described as textbook. I was reassured by his regular, even breathing as he slept, oblivious to our struggles.

The clock ticked as lunchtime came and went and Arthur's shift at the local factory approached. My mind was numb with the sheer monotony of attempting to get the ends to meet and it wandered to thoughts of replacing prolapses in cows, which, until now, I had found arduous.

Nothing could compare to the numbing of my fingers and the strain over neck and back, or the cramped thumbs that finally led to the two ends of the fracture eventually being hauled, not into a perfect fit, but to some sort of alignment. Arthur was by now anxiously watching the clock and despite my exhaustion, I was aware not only of the fact that I was soon going to lose my assistant, but also of the length of time that Boris had been anaesthetised.

At least the next part of the surgery I had done before on the course, but it took every last ounce of energy to drill the nine-millimetre stainless steel pin from the fractured end up the shaft of the fracture, until it protruded out at the top of the leg. I cut a small incision to allow the pin to pass out through the skin and continued drilling it up until the other end was just protruding at the fracture site. Both the sheer size and the amount of swelling of the leg made it impossible for me to assess if my pin placement had avoided the sciatic nerve that ran behind the femur, but by now that seemed the least of my worries. With my gleaming new bone clamp holding the two ends of the fracture in rough alignment, I then drilled the pin back down the length of the leg into the second half of the bone. Using an identical pin, I was able to measure how far up the shaft the pin had travelled until it seemed to be in the right place.

Despite the pain deep in my back and shoulders and the fact that I was drenched in sweat, I felt a sneaking sense of triumph through my exhaustion. Cautiously, I moved the part of the pin that was protruding from the top of the leg and noticed how the entire leg now moved as one unit when I angled the pin. The leg was now, relatively, back in one piece.

'So. That's it, then,' announced Arthur, sounding glad that the ordeal was almost over.

'Well, now I just have to put the cerclage wire around the oblique edges.'

He couldn't hide his dismay and shifted awkwardly for a few more minutes until, looking pointedly at his watch, told me that he had to go to his shift in the factory.

'I didn't think it would take this long or I would have asked Seamus to swap with me,' he ended apologetically.

'Neither did I,' I replied wearily, wondering as I did if the pin would hold without the three cerclage wires. Reluctantly, I dismissed the thought, knowing that in such a big dog, the repair wasn't going to be ideal even with the wires.

As I cut the first length of wire, Arthur flushed the surgical site with several sixty-millilitre syringes of heated saline. The muscle around the site was beginning to take on a blueish tinge that worried me.

Then, with Arthur gone, a renewed flush of weariness washed over me, dissipating my momentary triumph. By now, I wasn't surprised to find that it wasn't as easy as I had thought it would be to angle the wire placer under the fractured shaft of the bone before threading the stainless steel wire through. The weakness that seemed to have taken me over made it difficult to pull the thick wire through the curved instrument. With the wire finally in place, I took up the wire twisters and, remembering the detail in the notes, I twisted the two ends of the wire around each other, leaving loop after loop, until the loops were down to the level of the bone. I cut the wire, leaving three loops to ensure the knot wouldn't open. The next wire was slightly easier to place and, as I tightened it, I began to feel that my ordeal might finally be coming to an end. As I readied myself to cut the wire, I gave one last twist to ensure it was tight enough, and watched in dismay as the wire snapped. I didn't even have the energy to berate myself as I wearily threaded through yet another loop until the second and third wires were finally placed.

The leg was by now unrecognisable and far from the perfect limb it had once been. I flushed the open wound with the syringes that Arthur had left for me and began what should have been the simple task of suturing back in place the layers of muscle and skin. Although it was technically easy, my numbed fingers fumbled with the instruments as I rejoined the muscle masses. It seemed like the edges of skin would never be sutured. As I placed the last knot, despite my exhaustion, I felt a slight tremor of hope and elation that, despite all, I had succeeded in doing what, on a few occasions, looked like being hopeless.

All that remained, now, was to cut the pin that protruded from the top of the limb.

With the glimmer of hope that came from completion, I giggled as I recalled my trip to the local hardware store two days previously to purchase the bolt crops that I knew would be necessary to cut the stainless steel pin. Molly, as usual, was familiar with the case in progress having met Boris on her frequent trips to the surgery. She had nodded knowingly as I held her up to the x-ray viewer and showed her where we would put the pin into the shattered leg and cut off the bit sticking out at the top. In fairness to the man in the hardware shop, I could hardly blame him as he observed a heavily pregnant woman arriving, with toddler in hand, when he asked what my husband needed the heavy-duty bolt crops for. Before I managed to reply, Molly, with her usual enthusiasm for the job, informed him that I needed it 'to cut the doggie's leg off'. Somewhere in her two-year-old brain, the story had got jumbled. I'm quite sure that the man thought that I was some psychotic hormonal female who was going off to commit some heinous crime. It took two more hardware shops to locate the required instrument that would be strong enough to cut the nine-millimetre stainless steel pin.

Somehow, the bolt crops seemed heavier now as I lifted them up to the level of the table before placing the jaws around the pin as close to the leg as possible. When I was finally happy with the placement, I braced myself to lever together the two jaws to cut the pin. My best efforts only left a scratch and I re-angled them again to get a better grip. Fifteen minutes later, I was still at it, but by now was standing on the operating table, one foot on either side of Boris, having decided that some extra height might give me a better chance. It was at that moment that Seamus chose to appear, irate from a stressful morning of awkward clients. Had I not been so tired, I might have laughed at the look of utter bewilderment as he observed me in full surgical garb, standing straddled over the prostrate body of the huge dog, brandishing my bolt crops. He watched and stared, until finally he begrudgingly asked, 'Do want a hand or is that the way you usually do it?' Too exhausted to care, I handed over my weapon and watched, as with one quick heave, he closed the jaws and the end of the pin shot off to the far corner of the room.

Never a man of many words, he watched silently as I undraped the dog and cleaned the site. He busied himself around the office as I waited for Boris to wake up sufficiently to remove the endotracheal tube. Only then did he return and, without a word, lift Boris off the table and put him in the kennel that I had readied with thick bedding and a heat lamp.

Unceremoniously I dumped my orthopaedic instruments into a sterilisation solution and cleared the worst of the mess while waiting for the kettle to boil. Because of the pain relief I had given him, Boris whimpered only slightly and recovered remarkably quickly from his lengthy anaesthetic. Wearily, I gulped a cup of tea and instantly felt nauseous as the milky liquid hit my stomach. I abandoned the remainder and went to adjust the flow rate on Boris's fluids.

I could never have imagined that one operation could take quite so much out of me and was relieved that I wasn't on call that night. Arthur promised faithfully to keep an eye on Boris, so it was the next morning, after a surprisingly deep sleep, that I was able to see how Boris was coping with his amateur repair. The first thing I noticed was that he placed his foot, although tenderly, to the ground – so at least I had managed to avoid the sciatic nerve with the pin.

Never having pinned a leg before, I was frustrated that I

didn't know what to expect and neither did anyone else in the practice. At least I was grateful that I wasn't having to reassure an anxious owner that everything was going well and the recovery was as expected. Or was it? I really had no idea.

The day of the surgery was my last week at work before going on maternity leave. On the Friday afternoon, with some difficulty I loaded Boris into the well-padded back seat of my car while Slug hauled herself into her customary position in the front seat. She sulked the whole way home, studiously ignoring our passenger. Molly was naturally delighted to have Boris, especially as his post-operative care consisted of several slow lead-walks a day – at just about at the speed of the average toddler. We became a common sight over the days that followed, Molly and Boris and me, pacing up and down the country roads. Despite the fact that Boris was putting some weight on his injured leg, the muscles continued to fade over the next few weeks, but he always enjoyed his walks and suffered no obvious pain.

With my baby's arrival well overdue and with Boris's regular walks now setting off some increasingly regular contractions, I finally handed him over to Catherine in the local welfare group, along with a list of instructions. I may have been over-meticulous with my list, but I thought that I should cover every eventuality. Arthur had agreed to take any follow-up radiographs and whatever else might be needed. I knew from experience that Catherine was thorough, even to the extent of being over-cautious, and thought she would be the ideal person to take over his care, given the severity of Boris's injuries.

It wasn't until the third phone call by lunchtime on the first morning that I was beginning to realise that Catherine was perhaps cautious to the extent of being over-zealous. By tea-time, I wished I had never handed him over, as it would have taken less time to care for him myself than field the barrage of phone calls relating to every aspect of his daily movements.

Whether it was from Molly's insistence that we carry on with the regular walks, with or without Boris, or the stress of answering the phone calls all day, it was only two days before I ended up in the local labour ward. In true form, Catherine rang while I was on the way in, concerned that Boris has taken a brief sniff at his leg before getting up, something she was quite sure he hadn't done on any other occasion. I casually mentioned my destination and suggested, feeling incredibly guilty towards my unfortunate colleague, that she ring Arthur if she had any more queries.

It came to a head in the labour ward when the phone rang for the third time; yes, it was Catherine, clearly distressed, trying to glean further snippets of information before I became unavailable. Niamh, the angel-faced but world-wearied midwife, grabbed the phone from me before I had a chance to answer. 'For God's sake, the woman is in labour. D'ye understand me? She's trying to have a baby, if you'd just let her get on with it.' With that she pressed end, switched off the phone and placed it on the nearest counter, well out of my reach, before returning to me with a menacing frown.

'Are you sure that was her again?' I muttered weakly, afraid to argue.

'Well, sure, what harm if it wasn't. I wasn't telling lies when I said you're supposed to be having a baby.'

With the interruptions halted, baby Fiona arrived in due course, much to the delight of her now big sister. Molly was happy enough to substitute daily walks of Boris with walking 'Nona', as she proudly introduced her baby sister to anyone we met.

I assumed it had been Catherine who had been ordered off the phone by the midwife as the silence from that front was deafening ever since. I was terrified to ring and enquire about Boris.

As baby 'Nona' progressed from sleeping two hours at a go to twenty minutes at a go over the following weeks, it was in the back of my mind that it must be getting near time to radiograph Boris's leg to see if the fracture was healing. But I was still afraid to ring, hoping that no news was good news.

This time my luck was out. Arthur arrived at the house one day with the sheepish look of a middle-aged bachelor visiting a woman with a new baby. I laughed to see him standing at the front door with a bunch of supermarket flowers and a beany baby tvoy still bearing the logo of the drugs company that had supplied a batch of vaccines!

Molly, who had long since appointed herself as official receiver of Fiona's presents, was more than happy with the offering and content to amuse Fiona with it.

It wasn't until the second cup of coffee that Arthur brought up the subject of Boris. He avoided my eye as he casually mentioned that he had had a phone call from Catherine one evening. Boris, it seemed, had been feeling well in himself and in his revived exuberant form decided to join Catherine when she went out to feed two yearlings she kept in her back field. I had given strict instructions that Boris was to have short but regular lead-walks only, as much from my lack of faith in my surgery as anything else. This day, however, she had let him off the lead and he had galloped the length of the field with the two frisky colts. Apparently, one of the colts had lashed out, catching Boris on his injured leg and Catherine had arrived at the surgery with Boris in a very distressed condition.

Faltering slightly, Arthur went out to his van and returned with a radiograph, clearly labelled with the practice stamp and Boris's name. I sat, stunned, looking at the perfect image of a leg with the pin snapped in two at the point of the fracture. The ends of the bone had overridden, and despite the evidence of a significant amount of healing callus at both ends, were now clearly fractured again.

I looked from the radiograph to Arthur. His face said it all.

'He's gone isn't he?' I demanded.

Arthur nodded.

'Did you put him down?' I asked, already knowing the answer.

Although I would never know if the story about the horses was true or not or whether the pin had just snapped while Boris was sleeping peacefully in his kennel, I knew for sure that my first orthopaedic case had well and truly failed.

CHAPTER FIFTEEN

THE WHITE STUFF

Ireland was playing France in a friendly at Lansdowne Road and the rain howled around the Kylemore roundabout.

'You know,' I said to Eamon, 'we just might get out early tonight.'

'Ah, don't say that,' he replied with the superstition of a born and bred Dub. 'Sure, you know we never get out on time.' After a few seconds of silence he continued, with a glimpse of pure hope on his face, 'But wouldn't it be marvellous to get to see the second half?' A look of desperate anticipation came from one who had served his time for over forty years of Blue Cross clinics that ran at prime football time, resulting in him missing more matches than he cared to remember.

'Okay, a rush job it is,' I declared and dispatched the first few drowned-rat-like dogs and their bedraggled owners in record time.

'Another few just arrived,' commented Eamon, peering

out the steamed-up window. 'No rush, though. Take your time,' he added, after another hasty look at his watch.

Sadly though, not everyone was interested in the match, nor bothered by the weather, 'Ah sure, I had te do somethin' te ge outa de house,' declared one football widow who had chosen the night to request a thorough analysis of her dog's chronic skin condition.

'You're marvellous, really, to take such good care of him,' Eamon told her through gritted teeth as he helped her down the slippery steps, while Gordon grinned at me, mentally preparing himself to catching just the highlights.

It was almost looking like it just might happen when there was a bit of commotion from the crowd. A taxi pulled up and out of it came a middle-aged man, staggering under the weight of a Golden Retriever-type dog. A rough bandage covered the dog's forelimb and the deep crimson staining made the extent of his injury fairly obvious. Eamon hurried them through the waiting crowd, the unwritten triage system kicking in as effectively as in any Accident and Emergency department.

'I'm glad yez was here tonight,' gasped the man as he relieved his burden onto the consulting table. 'De kids took him out for a walk. They never miss a day. Imagine bringin' a dog out on a day like this,' he said nodding towards the menacing sky. 'Said he jumped into de river at the park and came out like dis – musta stood on a bit o' glass or somethin'.'

I let him talk as I assessed the dog's condition. His gums were slightly pale and the heartbeat was rapid, although strong and regular. Gordon restrained the wet, shivering, blood-stained creature, hugging him closely, regardless of his own clothing, as I began to peel off the heavily sodden bandage through which blood was still dripping.

'I dunno 'bout takin' dat offa him, luv,' the man cautioned me. 'By God, der was blood everywhere. Lucky me mate 'as a taxi. I dunno who else wudda given me a lift.'

'Don't worry,' I assured him, 'I'll just have a quick look to see how much damage has been done.'

It took some time to unravel the layers of socks, a tie and some other unidentifiable material within which the leg was enclosed.

'You did a good job with the bandage, anyway,' I congratulated him, wondering to myself when the layers would come to an end. Finally, I pulled off the last blood-soaked pad but just as quickly clamped it back on again as a jet of blood shot out from the wound, liberally spraying the drugs cabinet that stood behind us.

'Oh! You're right. It is a bad one,' I agreed, frantically wondering what to do next within the confines of our mobile clinic. This was no case to be sent home with a few tablets and referred on to the local vets in the morning. 'I think we'll have to send you in to the emergency clinic with him,' I told the concerned owner. 'The cut itself, as much as I saw of it, doesn't look too bad but he has severed a blood vessel and that's going to need to be operated on tonight.'

While I worked on rebandaging the wound tightly enough to control the bleeding, Gordon explained about the emergency clinic. 'The Dublin vets don't do their own out-of-hours work anymore. They are all covered by a central on-call clinic. But you'd better bring you wallet with you,' he joked.

At that, the man looked genuinely downcast. 'Are yez talking much?' he asked. 'I did me back in last year – had an accident on the building site. Missus does wha' she can, but we've the three young wans at home. Even if I had the money, I couldn't afford te spend it on the dog, much an all as 'e's one of us.'

It was a dilemma. To control the bleeding, the bandage needed to be on very tight, effectively cutting off the blood supply to the limb. By morning, when the vets at the local veterinary clinics would be available to treat the dog at a discounted rate through the Blue Cross, the limb, deprived overnight of blood supply, would be dead.

I could see the anguish in the owner's face as he considered his options. The dog lay quietly, a little too quietly, silken head resting on Gordon's shoulder as we contemplated his fate.

'Is there nowhere else at all open tonight?' implored the man as much to himself as anyone.

Subconsciously, both Eamon and Gordon turned their eyes towards me. With a sense of doom that had nothing to do with the certainty that I was going to miss the match, I reluctantly muttered, 'Well, unless you can make your way down to Wicklow ...'

'Wicklow?' He jumped at it instantly. 'What's down in Wicklow?'

'Oh, a much better class of a practice, altogether,'

grinned Gordon. 'All the better vets are based in Wicklow!'

'And do you think they'd take him?' asked the client hopefully.

'Well, ask her yourself,' replied Gordon, nodding at me.

Before we moved on to the next patient, Harry had directions to the practice and we had exchanged mobile numbers. 'I'll ring you as soon as I get finished here and you can meet me down at the clinic,' I told him.

Off he went to try to borrow a car for the journey as his taxi friend had long since left. Despite the delay, we finished not long after eight, a minor miracle for the clinic. Eamon and Gordon were sure to catch at least the second half of the match.

With the usual weariness that hits at the end of any day, I was beginning to regret my offer. I rang Harry to tell him I was on my way, but he told me that he still didn't have a car organised. Had there been any other option, I would have switched off my phone and headed home, but I just couldn't abandon this poor dog.

Donal wasn't too happy when I rang to tell him I'd be late. 'Do you know this guy at all?' he asked, sounding concerned. 'What are you going to do with him while you're operating?'

To be honest, I hadn't thought that far ahead. 'Well, he'll just have to go home. He can collect the dog in the morning,' I replied, suddenly none to keen to have this total stranger waiting with me late at night in the surgery.

'What did Seamus think?' he asked, as usual way ahead of me in terms of practicalities.

'Sure, we'll see what he says in the morning,' I replied,

to tired to worry about it.

I was almost half-way home when Harry finally rang me back. 'I'm sorry, luv, but I'm on me way now. Had te borrow de taxi offa me mate. Was waiting for 'im to come back from a run te de airport. Sure, I'll not be long after ye.' His mate was obviously a generous type. I hoped there weren't a few speeding points clocked up on Harry's licence – he arrived at the surgery while I was still setting up.

As soon as he had signed the consent form, I ushered him back out the door, conscious of being alone in the practice with this total stranger.

'You can pick him up at nine in the morning,' I told him, opening the door for him.

For the second time in an evening, his face dropped.

'Nah, luv,' he told me. 'I've te get de taxi back te me mate. He's te be back on his run in de mornin'.'

No amount of persuasion would induce him to leave the dog with me and I was starting to despair at my moment of weakness back at the clinic, determining, yet again, never to get involved in anything like this again.

Even the threat that he could be waiting until three in the morning until the dog was sufficiently awake to travel home didn't bother him.

'Dat's no problem, a' all, luv,' he assured me. 'I'm just so delighted to 'ave 'im looked after.'

Happy and all as he was to stay until three in the morning, I had no intention of it. Cringing as I thought about how Seamus would react, I opened a bottle of the expensive intravenous anaesthetic that I had talked him into stocking for sick or high risk (and preferably paying) patients. For the job on hand, it did have the added advantage of offering a very fast recovery time.

'Would you mind holding him while I inject this into the vein?' I asked, hoping that Harry wasn't going to get squeamish at this stage.

'Not at all,' he assured me, confidently. 'You just tell me wha' ye want me te do and I'll do it.'

He was as good as his word, but once Charlie was peacefully sleeping and drawing even, measured breaths on the gas machine, I thanked him for his help and led him back out to the waiting room.

I was little bit on edge, operating late at night, especially as Slug, who would normally accompany me on late-night calls, was sleeping peacefully at home, Ballyfermot being her night off.

The procedure itself was effortless – the most demanding part being the cleaning of the matted blood off the surrounding fur. Having tied a tourniquet above the wound, I was able to remove the bandage and ligate the bleeding vessel with a small section of catgut. Having tied it off, I cauterised the end of the vessel to ensure that it would not start to bleed again. A quick exploration of the wound revealed no further damage. I flushed a quantity of saline over the wound to remove any contamination and two simple sutures closed the innocent-looking cut that had caused me such grief. Within minutes of turning off the gas in the anaesthetic machine, Charlie was sitting up, and his feathery tail wagged lazily, confirming that all was well in his world.

'How's Charlie?' asked Harry, jumping up out of his chair as soon as I came through. He was stunned to see him follow behind me, slightly wobbly, but otherwise clearly well.

'Yer man was righ' when 'e said dat yez are better vets down 'ere. De look o' him is worth de drive.'

By then, I was too tired to appreciate his approval, especially as I would have to explain myself to Seamus the next morning. Having let Harry out and loaded Charlie back into the taxi, I locked myself back in the surgery and did a quick clean-up, even stopping to scrub and repack the suture kit which I wouldn't normally bother to do at this hour of night. It was well past midnight when I finally got home to bed.

I was always tired on a Thursday morning and the next day was no exception. It seemed I wasn't the only one who was having a bad day. Seamus was in one of his rare foul humours. He hadn't seemed to notice anything amiss and I diplomatically decided not to fill him in at that moment. I felt a bit bad, but used the donation which Harry had given to cover the cost of the drugs and materials I had used.

Nothing was said and it looked like I had got away with it. By Friday morning, I had almost forgotten about my venture and I was delighted to see that Seamus was back to his usual form.

'Gillian, you're looking a bit tired today,' he informed me jovially, as I arrived in. 'All the late nights catching up on you?'

I looked at him, feeling slightly perplexed. Sometimes

his good moods were almost as hard to fathom as his bad ones.

'Sure, it's been fairly quiet lately. No late nights at all, apart from Molly and Fiona,' I replied, genuinely forgetting about my mid-week surgery.

'Ah well, at least the children must appreciate you just as much as your clients do,' he laughed gaily.

I was almost out the door when he called me back. 'Oh, I nearly forgot! Some post arrived for you today. Sorry – it was addressed to the practice so I opened it.'

'What a cute little puppy,' he added, feigning a most uncharacteristic interest in the chocolate-box style puppy on the front of the card.

I was perplexed – the local cattle farmers weren't overly prone to sending thank you cards in grateful receipt of a good job. All was to be revealed as Seamus stood, theatrically, to read out the card to me.

Dear Gillian,

Just to let you know how grateful we were to you for stitching up our dog Charlie on Wednesday night. There's no way we could have afford to pay a real vet out in Dublin. That white stuff you injected into the vein to make him go asleep was deadly. There's not a bother on him at all now – probably from all those great painkillers and stuff you gave him. Hope the boss wasn't too annoyed.

Thanks again, from all the gang on
Cherry Orchard Drive.

'Excellent work,' finished Seamus, dripping with heavy sarcasm. 'I always knew you'd pull the business in. And you were right! It's well worth stocking those expensive anaesthetics for our valued clients. Keep up the good work,' he added magnanimously, before sweeping out the door.

CHAPTER SIXTEEN

A TEMPERAMENTAL
VEHICLE

I t seemed that fate was against me in my resistance to investing in a tax-efficient jeep. My well used, or more likely, abused, car was delivered to the garage not long after my meeting with the accountant for a much overdue service. I always hated anyone other than myself having anything to do with the car as it meant emptying everything out of it. This process started with the front seat, removing Slug's blanket and making a futile attempt to hoover out the coarse grey hair that seemed to have stitched itself into the material. Then on to the back, removing Molly and Fiona's car-seats, along with a selection of toys, soothers, bottles, nappy bags, changes of clothes, squashed crisps and other often unidentifiable objects. Once the main part of the car was emptied, it was on to the boot, which had to be relieved of a wide variety of drugs, equipment, needles, syringes, wellies, overalls and all the paraphernalia of veterinary life.

The ominous phone call came a few hours later.

'Do you really drive that thing?' an amazed voice came over the phone. 'It's a bloody death trap!' Apparently, the intermittent wobbles and squeaks and shudders that accompanied our daily voyaging indicated that the suspension in the car was pretty much non-existent. But our last journey had passed – the local mechanic, who was a friend of the family, insisted that I hold on to the car he had lent me until I got something else.

Squashing everything into the borrowed car was a bit of a challenge, especially while trying to keep the mashed crisps and Slug's hair out of the unfortunate vehicle which, judging by its pristine condition, was used to a more glorious vocation.

On the third day, Donal rang me with the details of a few cars he thought might be worth a look, including an ex-demo model jeep. Little did I know how much I would come to hate that jeep!

I took an afternoon off work to go around the garages. Piling everything in and out of the car further emphasised how time was not on my side. I quickly passed over the first two cars – one was so outrageously expensive that it would have written off my annual wages along with my tax bill, while the other had a boot that the calving jack could only fit in at an angle. Arriving into the showrooms of the third garage, I was greeted by a small, besuited man, who promptly proffered the proverbial wet fish handshake and told me that my husband was happy with the jeep so I needn't be too worried about it. Having inspected the size of the boot to ensue it was big enough to fit all I required, I asked if we could take it for a test drive. The salesman looked decidedly uncomfortable as I began to load Molly and Fiona, complete with car-seats, into the back. It was only as I called Slug out of the front seat of the car that he really started to perspire.

'The dog can stay in your car until we get back,' he hurriedly told me as I called her around to the passenger seat. Slug snuffled around the gleaming tyres with nonchalant interest.

'If you don't mind,' I told him, 'I'd rather bring her with us. She'll be spending as much time in the car as I will.'

'But this is a relatively new vehicle, with fully upholstered seats, alloy wheels, the lot. You surely aren't going to let your dog into it?'

'Look,' I said, turning to him, 'it's very simple. My dog is part of my job. If she can't climb into the jeep without me lifting her in, I won't buy it. She might not look big, but she weighs over twenty kilos and I can't spend the day lifting her in and out after each call. If she can't come with us then there's no point in me looking at it. I won't waste your time any further.'

He continued to stare incredulously at me until I turned and began to undo Molly's straps.

'Okay then,' he burst out. 'But if she dirties it or something, I'll have to charge you a soiling fee.'

'Does that apply to the dog and the children or just the dog?' I asked sweetly before turning to open the door for her. 'Come on, Slug,' I encouraged.

Despite the cushiness of her current job, Slug's dubious

past was inclined to catch up on her when it came to any form of athletics. Her early days of neglect and malnutrition meant that it was only with difficulty that she could jump any height at all, unless there was a feathered, warm-blooded object in view. Cautiously, she surveyed the step into the back seat.

'Sluggy! Sluggy!' called Molly from the heights of her car seat, enthusiastically banging her opened palms on her knees. Twice Slug made to jump, but chickened out. The salesman continued to stare in disbelief as Molly and I encouraged Slug to climb up the step. Even Fiona broke into shrieks of excited laughter when Slug finally hunched down on her bum and made the leap, quivering with as much concentration as it might take to face the highest jump in the RDS.

With Slug safely inside, I strapped myself in the driver's seat while the pale-faced salesman got in the other door.

'I'll just show you how to use the gear box, then,' he began breathlessly, clearly not enjoying the trip.

'No need, thanks,' I told him. Having spent a few winters in the heights of Glencree, I had become fairly adept at fitting snow chains and altering gear boxes when the need arose.

To me, not being a car freak, the jeep was just like any other to drive, apart from being nice and clean at the moment – but that, I knew, wouldn't be for long.

After a few minutes, I got bored with the stony presence beside me and swung up by the Greenhills road to return to the garage. It was only as we pressed our way through the steady traffic that I noticed a familiar odour emanating from behind us. Obviously Slug was passing off the gaseous remains of the chicken curry we had shared for supper the previous evening on the way home. I glanced subtly sideways to see if my passenger had noticed and by the contortions in his face was left in no doubt that he had.

'I think one of the girls needs a nappy change,' I said casually, smiling encouragingly at him, mentally apologising to both Molly and Fiona for the subterfuge.

By the time we got back to the garage, the smell was more or less gone. Nonetheless, the salesman was out the door like a shot, without a word.

Despite his lack of sales skills, I decided that I would have to buy the jeep, and I rang the garage the next morning to ask them when it would be ready.

'Well, we will have to valet the jeep before it can go so I suppose you can pick it up tomorrow,' the girl on the desk informed me.

'I suppose I might as well let them hoover Slug's hairs out for the last time,' I told Donal later that evening, with a laugh.

Unfortunately, for me, it was the last laugh I was to have with that jeep.

I should have suspected on the night we collected it that the jeep was not going to be lucky for me. On that very first evening as we drove over the mountains through a heavily wooded area, a figure dived off the bank out of nowhere, catching the front light and bumper. Thankfully, with the weight of the jeep, the impact was not what it might have been, but it took a few seconds before I figured out what had happened. In the light from the headlamps, one of which was now smashed, I could see a six-pointer stag looking slightly dazed in front of us. As it was not even the rutting season, when hormonal males are prone to doing unusual things, I could see no logical reason as to why the stag had chosen to jump down the bank just at that very moment or whether he had intention-ally planned to head-butt the jeep. In the few seconds that it took us to gather ourselves, the stag regained his compo-sure and with a shake of his head, pranced off over the opposite ditch.

Naturally, the acquisition of the jeep led to much slag-ging from the farmers.

'Thought the bills had gone up a bit, all right!' said one.

'No wonder you want us to vaccinate the cows – sure, you need something to pay for that yoke,' said another.

Definitely, it was handy being able to drive across the field to the cow that was down, having calved in the far ditch, and when it came to being able to use the head-lights as the sole source of illumination for a caesarean on a heifer on the side of a mountain one evening, I was grateful.

On the other hand, however, it seemed that I had been landed with a jeep that was downright unreliable. It started with the electrics. When I turned on the windscreen wipers, the headlights went off – not ideal when heading at speed up a twisty mountain road. When I opened the electric window, the alarm went on – and wouldn't go off again for the next hour and a half while I completed two calls and made my way, ears ringing, to the nearest garage.

Then I started having problems with the fuel tank.

Alarmed by the increase in my diesel bills, I started to record the fuel output. It seemed that every other day I was filling up the tank, which despite my heavy mileage seemed excessive. It wasn't until I noticed the telltale smell and the dark spot on recently vacated ground that I realised there was a problem. The garage from which I had bought the jeep was at best unsympathetic, at worst downright negligent. Being on call meant that it wasn't easy to get the jeep back to their garage, some seventy miles from the practice and they refused to let it be repaired anywhere else as it was still under warranty.

It was at least a week, and many tanks of diesel later that I finally headed back out there. Going around a roundabout, the jeep took a slide, which resulted in me doing a one hundred and eighty degree turn, ending up on the roundabout facing back the way I had come. Slug glared at me from where she had landed on the floor below the passenger seat.

The problem was finally revealed to be a leaking fuel pump that was allowing diesel to drip down over the back wheel, explaining my acrobatics on the road. The warranty covered the repairs, but not the fuel that I had lost or the two days it took to be repaired.

For the next three weekends that I was on call, the jeep broke down, leaving me stranded. By the end of spring, I was on familiar terms with every AA mechanic in Wicklow. Two more fuel tanks were replaced and a few more repairs, the explanations for which were lost on me. On one occasion (it happened to be Christmas) when I tried to make contact with the garage where I had the warranty, the recorded message stated that the garage would remain closed until the eighth of January, some twelve days away – so the local garage made a temporary repair. But then, when I brought the jeep back to the original garage, they claimed that the warranty was no longer valid as another garage had caused the faults. After that I gave up ringing them and rang the solicitors instead. A lengthy discussion followed involving many whithertos and wheretofores, leaving me with the impression that the solicitors were going to make a lot of money out of this and I was still going to be the loser. Before I had decided where to go with it all, the final straw came.

Des Leadon was not a farmer whose company I relished. On the first day I had set foot in his yard, he had looked me up and down and pulled the old pipe out long enough to utter, 'Ye'r from Dublin, are ye?' with a look of utter contempt. I knew, from that moment, that trying to create any sort of an impression was futile. In a way, it was just as well that I had abandoned my high hopes of impressing all my clients equally because over the months that followed, I became to Des what my jeep was to me. From that day on, everything I touched in Des's yard turned to disaster.

While I was handling some cows to see if they were pregnant or not, his best heifer took fright and reared up and out over the crush gate. She might have made it had she not caught her hind leg on the top rail, which snapped with the impact and stabbed into her abdomen. Luckily for her, she landed head first on the rocky surface and died with a few open-mouthed gasps, thankfully oblivious to the splintered plank impaled in her side. Although the fault was with Des's crush, he, of course, blamed me and was none too concerned that the heifer had managed to kick me on the way over, leaving a cloven-shaped hoof mark on my chest which passed through a variety of interesting shades before it eventually disappeared a good while later.

On the next visit, I had to carry out a caesarian section on an old cow. Despite my relief that the surgery had gone in textbook fashion, Des rang a week later, mumbling down the phone to Seamus that the cow had not only gone down that night and not got up since, but in going down, had sat on and killed the calf.

'Sure, maybe,' muttered Des to Seamus at the end of a litany of woes, 'if ye send that young wan out to put the cow out of her misery, the auld bitch might get up and walk – everythin' else that wan does goes arse-ways up.'

On my last visit, the task had seemed idiot-proof. A heifer calf had been delivered out of a good cow the previous week, but it was unclear from Des's dates whether he was the progeny of an expensive AI bull, which would have left the heifer potentially worth a lot of money, or if she was by the sweeper bull and therefore would be let off for whatever she would fetch at the local mart. To determine her parentage, my task was to pluck some hairs from her tail, seal the sample in a container and send it off to a lab, which, by means of DNA testing, would reveal the heifer's true value. Seamus admitted that when Des had rung to book the test he wasn't overjoyed to have me come out, but as the other vets were tied up with calls and he wanted to get the sample to the labs urgently, he reluctantly agreed.

On the way out to the calf pens, I noticed a large, rangy bullock isolated in a pen and thought that he was blowing a bit. Hoping, in some way, to redeem myself, I casually mentioned to Des that the bullock didn't look too good and asked if he would like me to take a look at him.

'Indeed and I do not,' he spat out at me. 'Isn't the poor divil bad enough without you gettin' yer hands on him.'

Stunned into silence, I said no more and we stomped out around the back of the shed to where my patient waited. Looking at the thriving calf, I felt confident that she was by the good bull, but decided not to offer any opinion. At least, I thought, for once there might be a positive outcome to my visit.

Having plucked the required sample, I carefully examined it to ensure that enough follicles were present. I then sealed and labelled it and I was thankful to get out of the yard in record time. Without a backward glance, I pulled out and went straight for the post office where, correctly labelled, the parcel was sent towards its destination. It was late that evening when I got back to the office but I wasn't surprised, with the time of year, to see Seamus's jeep still in the driveway.

Seamus seemed in a peculiar mood, but with a load of reports still to be filled in, I didn't pay too much attention to him, hoping to get my paperwork completed before the evening clinic.

After a few minutes he casually mentioned that he had been talking to Des that afternoon.

'Oh great. Lucky you,' I replied, not taking my head out of the sprawl of paper. 'Giving out about me as usual, I suppose? At least I can't be blamed for killing anything this time – he wouldn't even let me look at a sick bullock he had in the yard.'

Surprised not to get some reply, I looked up at Seamus, who was still standing, watching over my shoulder.

'Well,' he continued after a lengthy pause. 'He did mention that the calf died after you left.'

'Yeah, very funny,' I replied, unconcerned. 'Well, if that bullock dies, he needn't blame me.'

After a pause, Seamus continued. 'I'm not joking. The calf did die. Apparently it dropped dead about twenty minutes after you left the yard.'

Somehow, by some freak of nature, it appeared that a healthy, thriving calf had let out one great big bellow and dropped dead for some unknown reason, which in all reality could never have had any connection whatsoever to me plucking a few hairs out of his tail. Until the day Des Leadon dies, he will never be convinced of anything other than that I killed his calf. Of course, in typical sod's law fashion, when the DNA results came back, they proved that my casualty was, indeed, a very expensive one.

From that day on, I tried my best to avoid the yard but my luck was to run out one weekend when I was on duty. Just after midday, a call came in to say that one of Des's cows was down with milk fever. As I was the only vet on duty for the day there was no option but for me to attend.

'At least,' I consoled myself, 'it's only a milk fever. What could go wrong?'

Milk fever, a condition where the calcium in the body gets rapidly depleted from the high demands of milk production, results in a cow going down and even dying if treatment is not given quickly enough. However, once treated promptly, a simple bottle of the intravenous calcium will restore full health in a very short space of time.

'Yet,' I continued to myself, 'if that calf managed to drop dead …'

My sense of dread intensified as I neared my destination. Quickly, I rechecked the boot: several full bottles of calcium, a clean flutter valve, needles – everything was in order. I vowed to inject the cow and get out as quickly as possible. At least, even though it was my weekend on call, the jeep so far, for the first time in my previous four weekends on call, had not broken down. A man like Des would be convinced that a broken-down car would be yet more evidence of my inherent incompetence.

Soon we were passing through the nearby village and a sense of relief flooded though me, knowing that even if we broke down now, I could grab my gear and walk if necessary. Within a few minutes, I was pulling in through the gates of the yard.

Although Slug often came out in the yards with me, on this occasion, I told her to stay, whispering in to her through the opened boot, 'Don't worry, we'll be out of here soon.'

Having pulled on my wet gear, I left her gazing anxiously after me, sitting on the driver's seat, paws on the steering wheel.

Des managed not to utter a single word to me or make

any eye contact as we trudged though the mucky yard to the calving boxes where the cow lay.

Following his lead, I silently examined the cow, and indicated that I would return to the jeep to get the required calcium. In our college days we had always been advised to fully examine the patient before producing the appropriate medication.

Back at the jeep, I went to pull open the boot and was irritated to find it was locked. 'Bloody electrics,' I muttered to myself, knowing I had left it open.

It was only when I went around to the passenger door and found that it too was locked that I started to panic. Running around to the driver's seat, pulling in vain at the handle, I felt a wave of heat surge up through my body as I saw the car keys glisten against the bright spring sun, hanging smugly from the ignition. I was locked out. It was only after a minute or two that I realised that my initial reaction in blaming the electronics was incorrect. In fact, it was actually Slug who, obviously offended at having been left behind, had jumped from the passenger's seat to the driver's seat and inadvertently managed to stand on the control panel that lay between the seats, triggering the central locking. For a second, I thought of just getting into the jeep and driving away, as fast as I could, to somewhere, anywhere, preferably a few counties away, until I realised I couldn't even do that.

In a moment of brilliance, I decide that if Slug had managed to stand on the control panel while crossing over the seats, she could do it again and reverse the locking. As she now sat in the driver's seat, I ran around to the passenger's side and called her to me. She happily obliged, jumping cleanly over the control panel. Running back to the driver's side, I called her again. Another clear round! Back I ran to the passenger's side, desperation hitting. No joy! Around and back I ran, again and again, with Slug enjoying the game enormously.

It was this sight that greeted Des when he finally decided to come and see what had happened to me.

'Are ye playing with the dog or are ye going to treat me bloody cow?' he bellowed up the yard. It was the first time I had ever heard him speak in anything other than an undertone. I stared at him, like a rabbit caught in headlights and reluctantly stumbled out my story.

Out of the corner of my eye, I could see the shiny bottles of calcium ready and waiting to restore my dignity. For a moment, I wished I was back at my inner city clinic where surely some local youth would have gladly picked the locks for a fiver.

'I don't suppose you're any good at picking locks?' I trailed off as Des stared at me with disbelieving contempt.

Some forty minutes later, I was back at the yard, having had to endure sitting by Des's side in his car as we bumped our way to the surgery to collect a few bottles of calcium and a flutter valve. As he waited for me, Des sat sullenly staring into space. 'Are ye sure ye haven't forgot anythin' or would ye like me te have te drive ye back out again?'

It seemed a lifetime before I watched the sticky liquid flow into the blood stream, flicking determinedly at the valve to look like I was doing something. With a long, loud belch, the cow, staggering a bit, tucked in her hind legs and got up.

'Well, ye haven't killed her – yet,' Des informed me, back by now to his muttering as he shuffled off to the farmhouse.

I didn't see him again as I sat at the end of his long avenue until after lunch waiting for the AA to come and open the car. Slug, thoroughly bored by now of the game of running from one side to another, snoozed peacefully.

Ironically, the cow lived, and from that day on I had no more disasters, although Des never once gave me credit for anything I ever did.

I advertised the jeep in the *Farmer's Journal* the next week and ended up selling it for a few thousand euro less than I had paid for it not six months previously. I felt bad because I sold it to another vet from the far side of the country, but I knew he felt bad because he thought he had ripped me off. I heard a few years later, from a colleague who worked with him, that it had never given him a moment's trouble.

CHAPTER SEVENTEEN

THE BEWITCHING HOUR

Probably one of the most obvious life-style changes in veterinary practice, as well as life in general, is the total and unrelenting tie to a mobile phone. In many ways, the mobile phone is an invaluable tool for the provision of an emergency service, to the extent that it is often hard to imagine how our veterinary predecessors ever survived without them; but sometimes, just sometimes, how I envied my older colleagues their position. With the advent of mobile phones, every trace of privacy had been taken away. Now, it is possible for a client to ring the emergency number just as you are settling into a hot bath to ask what time your next surgery is at. Or they can ring you when you are pushing a laden trolley around the supermarket, complete with a collection of irate toddlers, to find out how much a vaccination is likely to cost. Better still, while sitting in church, where hopefully you have remembered to at least put the phone on vibrate, an inquisitive client can ring to query an account or double-check the dose of antibiotics. Once qualified as a veterinary surgeon with a mobile phone, your life, your plans, your next moves, are never your own. Everything is dictated by the whim of the person at the other end.

I noticed that every time the mobile rang out of hours, my stress levels jumped. For those few seconds, where the call could be from the owner of a seriously ill animal requiring major intervention, or from a client with not enough manners to realise that you might, possibly, be trying to have some sort of a life outside the job, the stress is huge. It was almost amusing at any veterinary gathering to observe how when a mobile rang, everyone responded in some way. For myself, I found that it helped me to change the ring tone every few months.

Within weeks of qualifying, I endured a particularly long night of almost continuous calls, almost all from the one client. It didn't help that the client in question was not, in fact, a client at all, but had been given the practice emergency number by Directory Enquiries. The first call came shortly after midnight, just as I had fallen into a deep sleep, exhausted by the demands of the work as a new graduate. Serena, my potential client, apparently did not occupy the same time zone as I did, as she sounded incredibly bright and cheery at the other end.

She explained at length how her little terrier didn't seem quite himself. In my zealous enthusiasm at the time, I grilled her in detail about the dog in question, but found that with her somewhat vague replies to my in-depth questioning, I was unable to fathom why she felt it necessary to call an emergency number after midnight. As the conversation continued, she seemed to lose interest in talking about the dog and I found myself continually trying to steer her back to the topic and away from discussion of a party that was going on in the flat above and the general comings and goings around her. It seemed, as far as I could gather, that the dog was doing everything a dog should be doing, other than the fact that his owner felt that he was not as bright as he should be.

By the end of our, by now, lengthy conversation, I still couldn't quite figure out why Serena was worried, but suggested that if she was still concerned in the morning she could bring him into the clinic for a check-up. At this she explained that she had no transport and would much prefer if I called out to her. 'I don't wanna be puttin' anyone ou' havin' te drive me over to ye. But don't come out in the mornin',' she concluded. 'Dis party will be goin' on all nigh' and I'm not workin' anyways, so I never wud be up before t'afternoon meself.'

At least this explained why she was so bright and happy, not having suffered from the ill-effects of a strenuous working day. She seemed reluctant to end the call, but, by now, I could barely keep my eyes open, knowing that it was clearly a false alarm. Thankfully, I settled back down into the bed, but couldn't go back to sleep, wondering whether, in my newness to the job, I had missed some vital piece of information.

It was only when I had finally drifted off, almost an hour

later, that the phone rang again.

'How're ye?' called out a familiar voice. 'It's me again.'

'Sorry, who am I talking to?' I asked, momentarily for-getting the previous call.

'It's Serena – the one wi' the dog, y'know?'

It seemed that my in-depth questioning had created a barrage of new concerns in Serena's over-alert mind that in her eyes needed to be dealt with and now she was ada-mant that she wanted me to call out – immediately – to examine her dog.

Again, doubting myself, I repeated my list of questions and my 'over the phone diagnosis' assured me that there was absolutely no indication, even in my over-anxious state of being a new graduate, to see the dog in any sort of a hurry. Politely, I explained myself, but by now Serena was becoming somewhat agitated and a little bit more aggressive than her previous chatty form. Several times she cut across me to give directions to one of the most dubious inner-city addresses. The place was familiar to me, as one of my very first calls in my new job had been to examine a horse for a welfare group in that very estate. The welfare organisation had advised me to ring the guards to accom-pany me for safety purposes. After two days of continuous requests at the local police station, I eventually went out on my own.

The third time Serena rang, I didn't have to ask who was calling. I could clearly hear the sound effects of the house party that was obviously now in full swing. Again I repeated my questions and again I reassured her that her little dog sounded perfectly healthy and his general well-being was of no immediate concern. There was no friendly banter from her this time and her verbal aggression made me glad I had refused to go out. This time I told her very firmly that I was not going out to see the dog and reiterated that she should attend the clinic the next day if she was still concerned.

I had only hung up when the forth call came – this time screaming abuse with no preamble. By now, it had begun to sink in that perhaps Serena's initial euphoria during the first call and her subsequent paranoia and now aggression were not entirely from natural causes.

The next few calls came in rapid succession; each time I simply repeated that I was not going to call out and told her not to ring again. Then, for a blessed two hours there was silence, but at that stage I was so agitated and bewildered that I tossed and turned, endlessly hoping, in vain, to sleep.

The alarm clock flashed four-thirty when the calls began again. Now there was crying and stories of an ex-boyfriend and an irate landlord and some neighbour who was causing trouble and wanting me to call out – and, this time, not even a mention of the dog. The next few calls continued in such quick succession that I eventually lost track of them; it was only the following morning that I counted a total of sixteen calls received from Serena.

Eventually, the calls slowed, with Serena becoming more and more disjointed. Then they stopped abruptly at about six-thirty in the morning. My head ached with weariness and frustration as the first burst of the dawn chorus assaulted my ears and I battled to sleep. I didn't ever find out what happened to either Serena or her dog, if she had one; since six-thirty that morning, I never heard another word from her.

When the phone shrilled in my ear again a little after eight that morning, I felt like a very taut wire. This was the seventeenth time in eight hours, and I snapped. Of course, the inevitable happened. Without even bothering to check the number flashing on the screen, I pressed Answer and bawled into the phone: 'Your dog is not sick. I am not coming out to see you. Don't ever ring this number again.'

I heaved a breath, exhausted with effort and stress. There was silence at the other end of the phone.

'Did you hear me?' I yelled, determined to make my point. 'Don't ever ring me again.'

Again, silence, followed by a very shocked and hesitant voice which sounded vaguely familiar. In disbelieving horror, I gradually recognised the subdued tones of one of my lecturers from college. I had referred a lame dog to him the previous week and he was ringing to report on the patient's progress.

But it seemed that he was now more concerned about me! My mind was so numb with mortification. It seemed so unfair that I could be caught out in that one off-guard moment.

'... and we all have bad days ...' I heard him say. 'And if ever you feel the need to talk ... And sometimes we find that veterinary is not the career we thought it would be ...' On and on he went while I lay back, burning a hole in the pillow with embarrassment and wondering if, within the cushy confines of the veterinary college, he had ever had to deal with sixteen calls between dusk and dawn from a client who was clearly in far greater need of help than her dog!

Although, thankfully, I've never had another night as bad as that one, there is no doubt that a considerable amount of stress comes from having to deal with night calls. At one stage, the clinic came up with the idea of diverting the phone to an answering service out of hours and during lunch time. With this, the client would have to leave a message with an unknown voice on a switchboard, who would then text a brief message to the vet on duty. As a rule, once clients realised that they were on to an answering service they would just ring back at a more appropriate time unless the call was urgent, in which case one of us would ring them back within minutes. We were all delighted with the idea initially, and for the first few nights it seemed to be a success. When unexpectedly encountering the paging system some people did leave messages about trivial issues, such as what time we would be answering the phone at, but we soon found that it was an effective device for training clients, though the receptionist did have to take a bit of flak when some didn't really grasp the idea of the pager service.

'That lad that answered the phone last night was no use at all,' boomed Jack O'Reilly over the phone at nine on the button one morning. 'I asked him how much pen strep to give me bullock and he told me he had no idea. Not much good to me at all.' We laughed to think of the poor guy sitting in his office getting entangled in a lengthy conversation with old Jack.

Unfortunately, our love affair with the paging system

was to come to an abrupt end. At almost two o'clock on a freezing cold winter's night, my pager beeped at the bedside. Slug snored on, not yet having identified the beeper as being a call. Fumbling over my bedside locker, I picked up the pager and read the message: Ring Mary Keogh. This was followed by a local number. Nothing more. No 'urgent'. No details.

In my groggy state, I was a bit confused by the message. The name was not familiar to me. Usually, the people in the pager service would add some bit of detail like 'cow calving' or 'dog hit by a car'. Before I had reached for the phone, the pager went off again, and then again – three messages in less than a minute. With a sense of dread, I realised that at this hour of night it had to be a calving or a colic or something that could not be dealt with by a reassuring phone call from the depths of the bed covers.

Having located the light switch, I scribbled down the number and before I had even dialled it, the message came through a fourth time. I'm never at my best when woken from a sleep, but four messages in a row were just a bit too much. Although this was some years after my night of hell with Serena, multiple calls still tended to cause me intense stress, and by the time my return call was answered, my blood pressure was rising.

'Gillian here, from the vet's,' I said curtly. 'What appears to be the problem?'

A voice even groggier than mine replied. 'Sorry, who did you say you were?'

'Gillian, one of the vets. You paged us four times. What is the problem?'

There was silence at the other end of the phone and then a mumbling and I could just about hear the muffled voice of a woman in the background.

'Who is it, Larry? Who's ringing at this hour of the night?'

More muffled sounds followed as I waited with increasing irritation, wondering what was going on. There was a pause before the man came back on the phone.

'Eem, yes, my wife did ring all right. She was just wondering at what age we could have our puppy vaccinated?'

The mixed emotions of relief that I didn't have to get out of bed and sheer outrage at someone ringing at two o' clock in the morning to enquire about puppy vaccinations swirled through me.

'You're joking!' I blurted out. 'This is an emergency service, FOR EMERGENCIES ONLY!' I had woken both Donal and Slug at this stage. 'Ring the office in the morning,' I snapped and just as I hung up I heard the man say, 'Well, thanks for returning the call.'

I was so furious at having been woken up that, ironically, I couldn't sleep. After about half an hour I got up and checked on Molly and Fiona, just for something to do, really. How I envied them their peaceful sleep – Molly, in characteristic head-under-the-covers mode, Fiona, fists tightly clenched as though concentrating on something really important. I'd say it was almost four before I nodded off into a fitful slumber.

The next morning, Arthur and Seamus were equally stunned when I relayed my tale. Melissa, the receptionist on duty, however, just started to grin as I got to the end of my story.

'You mean to say,' she asked, 'you rang them at two o' clock last night and ate them for asking about a vaccination?'

'Well, what would you expect me to do?' I asked, annoyed by her reaction.

'Well, it's just that the pager people rang first thing this morning,' she told me. 'They apologised profusely, but apparently there was some problem with the system and the pages were all delayed by twelve hours going out, and then they were all repeated three or four times from mid-afternoon onwards,' she finished, her face breaking into a grin as she watched me absorb this information. The shock must have registered on my face as it occurred to me that a twelve-hour delay meant that the unfortunate Larry and Mary Keogh had, in all innocence, left one perfectly reasonable message during lunch hour and been rung back in the middle of the night by an irate, neurotic vet, giving them a lecture about emergency services and out of hours calls!

* * *

Maybe it is just that in the twilight hours my tolerance dies somewhat or maybe the clients themselves become bewitched and lose some of their sense of normality. In the early hours of one Saturday morning, I got a call from a client – in fact, not a client, but a friend of a client, or actually, a neighbour who knew the friend of a client. I'm not sure exactly. Being woken from my sleep before dawn left my senses less able to follow the intricate details of how the person on the other end of the phone had come to ring me. Anyway, what evolved after a minute or two of such explanations was that the person in question had found a hedgehog. Glancing at my clock, I noticed that it was a little past three in the morning. 'You found a hedgehog?' I repeated incredulously, wondering had it just hopped into her room and appeared under the bedclothes or was she, perhaps, on an impromptu camping trip. 'Well, actually, I found him … or it could be a her – I'm not sure if it's a girl – last Thursday,' continued my newfound client. 'I found him under the garden shed. I think he was attacked by a cat or something.'

Thankfully, her continuous chatter prevented me from having to formulate any sort of reply as I lay slumped against my pillow. Briefly my eyes closed, before I awoke again with a jerk hoping to find out why she was ringing me at three in the morning about a hedgehog. It seemed she was finally getting to the point: '… and it's just that now he's making this sort of funny snuffling, grunting noise and I don't know what to do.' There was silence as I lay, phone to ear, wondering why it had to be me.

'Well,' I replied, thinking as ably as I could at that hour of the morning, 'I think that hedgehogs often make a snuffling, grunting noise. I wouldn't be too concerned. But if you are, why not keep him warm and safe in a box tonight and bring him into the surgery in the morning?'

'Oh, I couldn't do that, I'm afraid. I live in Kildare, you see. I just didn't want to bother my own vet at this hour of the night but Martina said you wouldn't mind me ringing you. There's no way I could get down to you in Wicklow. Is there any chance you could do a call-out?'

At least that hedgehog was alive at the time and may possibly have benefited from my professional services, although, I am sorry to say, my ethical conscience was not enough to convince me to make that trip to Kildare the next day. I never did discover the fate of the snuffling, grunting hedgehog.

Another night, however, was really to stretch me to my limits. It's not uncommon in the job to answer the phone to the sound of uncontrolled crying. All you can do is wait a few moments for the caller to identify themselves and give some clues so that you may offer some words of consolation or advice. After a few more, sobs, the strangled words came out. 'He got hit by a car ...' followed by more raucous crying. Instantly I woke up, now fully alert after a mere two hours of sleep. The combination of a road traffic accident and a hysterical owner normally results in work, be it minor or major. After a few questions, I realised I was getting nowhere. 'Can you put him in the car and bring him to the surgery?' I offered, hoping to at least get to the animal in question. In between the muffled sobs, I barely distinguished the words 'no car' and 'collect him'. Wearily, I realised that I was going to have to call out to collect the unfortunate animal, which would result in a lot of delay before getting it to the surgery for vital treatment. It was difficult to get directions from the lady herself and after a few minutes, I was passed over to an irate-sounding man who gruffly barked out directions to a housing estate some seven or eight miles away.

'I'll get to you as quickly as I can,' I told him, jotting down the last of the directions. 'In the meantime, keep him quiet and don't offer him anything to eat or drink.' There was a brief silence before the less devoted owner questioned, 'But how could he eat anything when he's dead?'

'He's dead?' I said, falteringly. Usually, the first few minutes of a phone call are taken up with discussion as to the clinical condition of the patient, but as the owner was so distraught I had by-passed that stage of the conversation and somehow missed this vital piece of information.

The silence on the other end of the line was unrewarding and again I repeated, 'So, he's dead?'

'Well, I said he's dead, didn't I? How dead to you want him?' at which a renewed wail broke out again in the background.

'I'm afraid,' I began, 'that if he's dead, then there isn't much point in me calling for him. There's really not a lot I can do.'

'Well, I can't have a dead dog in my garden. What am I meant to do with him?'

'Of course we can arrange to have him taken care of in the morning,' I continued, blissfully realising that I could stay in my bed for the moment. 'There is really no need for me to take him away at this hour of the night.'

'I didn't say anything about taking him away,' he bristled, clearly not pleased at my level of co-operation. 'The wife wants him buried in the back garden.'

I was momentarily stunned as it gradually dawned on me that this unknown man wanted me to call out his house and bury his dog in his back garden in the middle of the night. I was quite sure that there was never any mention of this level of care in the Hippocratic oath we once took.

'I'm afraid, Sir,' I replied, 'that really isn't part of the service we provide. It's not my job.'

'Well, it sure as hell isn't mine,' he roared back down the phone.

CHAPTER EIGHTEEN

NEW ARRIVALS

As soon as I palpated the solid, irregular mass deep in the cat's abdomen, I knew Sophie was in trouble. It was a Wednesday night and out in the clinic in Ballyfermot all had been going too smoothly for comfort. Until now, the patients had had nothing more than itchy ears, mild stomach upsets or the need for a routine vaccination. It almost looked like we were going to get out in time for Gordon and Eamon to catch the second half of Ireland versus Portugal on the big screen. The tall lady carrying a makeshift cat basket was second from last in the queue and it was only a quarter-past eight. Having struggled to open the straps on the box, she carefully folded back the edges of the lid to reveal a pretty little tortoishell cat, quite miniscule in stature. As she gently unwrapped the blanket, it was immediately obvious that Sophie was a very sick cat. Her eyes had sunk deep in their sockets and the protruding third eyelids were caked in a thick yellowish discharge. Her coat was dull and rough to the touch and from her hind quarters there came the ominous smell of a putrid discharge that stained both her fur and the blanket. Apparently, Sophie had happily delivered a litter of two kittens four days previously and, despite her tiny frame and tender age, all seemed well. When she became more listless, Sandra, the owner, had assumed that she was just settling peacefully into her role of motherhood, but then Sophie went off her food. For two days she had eaten nothing and only with great coaxing would she accept some warmed milk. It was the previous morning that the foul-smelling discharge had started and the owner knew that something was seriously amiss. Although the Blue Cross clinics operate from a different location every night at various centres around the city, Sandra herself had no car and had been unable to organise transport until that evening.

As Sophie was alone in the box, I assumed that the two kittens had not survived until Sandra dug deep in the pocket of her heavy overcoat and carefully pulled out two minute little creatures from what looked like a doll's blanket. At four days old, the kittens were pitifully thin, although they appeared to be fairly robust as they nudged at Sandra's outstretched hand, mewing piteously, desperate to procure some milk.

Running a hand along Sophie's tiny frame, I gently squeezed her mammary gland and was not surprised to find little milk.

'What is it? What do you think is wrong with her?' asked Sandra with obvious concern.

'I think she still has a kitten inside her,' I replied as I

gently probed the irregular mass in Sophie's abdomen.

'Oh, poor Sophie! What have I done to you?' asked Sandra, placing a protective hand over the tiny creatures in her hand.

'Can you do anything for her?' she asked eventually, as I stood silently examining the cat while my mind went over the limited options available.

'She needs to go on an intravenous drip tonight. She's much too sick and dehydrated for surgery at the moment. Hopefully, she may improve overnight, enough to operate on her in the morning.'

I could tell that Sandra wasn't really taking it all in. She glanced back at two young children who were waiting outside the tiny consulting area of the clinic.

'Will she make it, do you think?' she half-whispered to me.

'She is a very sick cat, but I think if we can start treating her tonight and then get her through surgery, she would have a chance. Cats are amazingly tough creatures,' I told her. I wondered, though, as I looked down at Sophie, who lay flat-out, oblivious to the consternation, her thin frame heaving with each laboured breath.

'I don't suppose you can do all that here, can you?' asked Sandra finally, a pleading look in her eyes.

'No. I'm afraid not. We really need to get her to the emergency hospital tonight.'

I knew as I said it that this just wasn't going to be an option. Sandra was a regular at the clinic as she suffered from a permanent disability that left her unable to work. Tending to the needs of her growing children stretched her meagre budget way beyond capacity. She would never be able to cover expensive bills for the family pet as well.

At that stage, Eamon discreetly went out with the children to distract them while I, Sandra and Gordon tried to come up with an alternative.

'How much would it cost me if we waited until the morning and I went to one of your referral clinics?' asked Sandra. The Blue Cross scheme usually paid half of the bill, but even with the discount I knew the cost would still be too much. Equally, I didn't think Sophie could wait until morning for treatment to begin if she was to have any chance of survival.

As I continued examining the fragile form on the blanket, I mentally re-ran Seamus's not so subtle displeasure the last time I had brought a Blue Cross case home with me, but still, I rationalised to myself, it's only a cat. It's not going to cost too much.

Knowing that there really was no alternative, I soon had Sophie and her kittens wrapped warmly in a cat cage I usually carried in the car with me. Sandra had signed a makeshift consent form and I promised to ring her in the morning as soon as the surgery was completed.

In the short time that the consultation had taken, the last remaining person in the queue had been joined by at least a dozen more. Before the next client came in, I got the litre of fluids I had stocked in my car and placed them in a sinkful of warm water. By the time the clinic was finally over, the fluids had heated and almost cooled down again. Gordon held the tiny kittens and Eamon held Sophie while I clipped and scrubbed a vein to insert an intravenous cannula. Sophie barely even registered the sharp needle piercing her tough, dehydrated skin and I sighed with relief as the plastic insert glided smoothly into the vein. Having securely taped the cannula in place, I attached the giving set and adjusted it to the correct rate. I then placed Sophie back in the cat carrier, along with her kittens. With the box secured on the passenger seat by the safety belt, I hooked the bag of fluids from the handle over the window, thankful for the thoughtfulness of car manufacturers in having included such a convenient drip stand!

I usually dropped Eamon home after the clinic and this time he was relegated to the back seat as we headed back towards the city.

On the way home, I toyed briefly with the idea of bringing Sophie into the practice, but apart from having to make the detour late at night, I realised that I had everything I needed for her in the boot of the car.

Slug was quite excited when I opened the door and she smelt the cat in the basket; even more so when she heard the snuffles and mews of the kittens. I set the basket up in the bathroom and while Donal boiled the kettle, I heated up a syringe of fluids for the kittens. Having swabbed their paper-thin abdomens with some antiseptic and then surgical spirit, I angled the needle through the skin and injected some heated glucose saline which would keep the kittens hydrated. In the morning, I would be able to get some kitten formula to add to the meagre ration they would receive from their mother.

Taking care to shut the bathroom door behind me, I took Slug out of temptation's way and settled down in front of the fire with a steaming mug of hot chocolate before climbing wearily into bed, hoping to catch a few hours' sleep before Fiona, now almost six months old, woke. She had developed a habit of waking up at wearyingly regular intervals with supposed colic throughout the night and I had long since given up on her 'growing out' of it. As usual, she first woke shortly after one in the morning and when she finally settled, I made my way down to check on the visitors, although there was not much that I could do for them at that stage. I repeated the procedure several times through the night, Slug snuffling enthusiastically behind me each time.

It seemed like I had only slept for half an hour when I became conscious of a tiny, solemn face staring intently at me from the bedside.

'Go back to bed, Molly. It's the middle of the night,' I muttered, hopefully.

It wasn't until I rolled over and saw that Donal's side of the bed was empty that I realised he had already left for work and it was now after seven.

Willing my eyes to open, I peered out at Molly. Happy that I was going to wake up she thrust her two arms towards me, clutching something in her hands.

'Have pussycat, Mammy!' she declared, opening her tiny fists to reveal the tiny tabby creature inside.

With a gasp of horror I sat upright, and made to take the kitten from her. Quickly, she closed her hands back over him and with the utter commitment of a two-year-old, said 'No, Monny mind him!'

Pulling her and her tiny charge up into the bed with me,

I sat and watched as she cuddled the little bundle into her, and with a gentleness surprising for a toddler, settled the kitten carefully into the folds of her fleecy pyjamas. Within seconds, the kitten's mewing subsided as he snuggled close into his minder.

Leaving her in the bed, I went back to the bathroom to check on the rest of the patients and was glad to see that Sophie, oblivious of the kidnapping that had taken place, was sitting up, still looking ill, but a little pit perkier than the previous night.

With Fiona now awake, I fed and changed her while Molly took charge of her 'babies'. When it was time for me to go to work, a tiny tear trickled down her face as I relieved her of the patients. It was only the promise that I would bring them all back that evening that enabled me to get away at all.

Down at the surgery, I was relieved to see that Seamus was going to be occupied for the entire morning with a big herd test. Other than that, there wasn't too much else on for the morning.

I quickly set up the operating table and once all was ready, attached a syringe containing the anaesthetic to the intravenous line. Sophie didn't budge as I depressed the plunger, but gradually her breathing became smooth and regular and her eyes took on a glassy appearance. It took longer than usual to clip and prep the scrawny little cat as her fur was matted with the putrid discharge. Once she was clean, I covered her with a sterilised drape and within minutes was making my first incision. Underneath the skin, the muscle was clearly visible, with little subcutaneous tissue to obscure my view. Picking up the midline with a forceps, I incised a tiny hole with the tip of my scalpel blade. Once through the gleaming peritoneum, I edged the tips of a surgical scissors into the opening and extended the wound until the problem was clearly visible. The uterus, five days after delivery, should be almost back to its own size. In Sophie's case, however, one horn still contained a long-since dead kitten. While one occasionally does have to remove dead kittens that are too big, or in the wrong position to be delivered normally, in Sophie's case it was something a little bit different. The uterus was partially obscured from view by the mesentery that connects all the organs in the abdomen. This tissue, usually white and glistening, was inflamed and angry-looking. Prising the damaged tissue carefully away from the horn of the uterus, it became all too clear why the body had reacted so violently. The smooth, glistening surface of the enlarged uterus was interrupted by a sharp object protruding out from the inside. Carefully, I incised over the mass to reveal another dead kitten, one that had died many weeks ago and become mummified in the once sterile environment of the uterus.

While the soft tissue had withered away, only the tiny bones remained. In attempting to deliver the tiny foetus, Sophie's contractions had forced the sharpened edges out through the wall, rupturing the uterus. Glancing at the shallow but regular breathing, I marvelled at how she had functioned as well as she had, considering the pathology inside. The natural attempt of the body to heal the damage by covering it with protective tissue had clearly failed.

Thankful that Sophie was a small cat and not a large, over-weight Labrador, I quickly set to the task of removing the uterus. Even if Sophie had been a prize pedigree, her breeding days were clearly now over. It was a relief to remove the distorted uterus knowing that she would never again have to go through the same ordeal.

Before the first call of the morning arrived in, I was placing the final row of sutures and admiring how a small, neat incision could hide what lay underneath.

While I was waiting for Sophie to recover from the anaesthetic, I fed the kittens again with some carefully mixed commercial kitten formula. When they were both content, I placed them in beside their mother under the heat lamp, bundling the entire family up within a fleecy rug. Before long, Sophie was sitting up groggily and then she turned to stare at her charges. Within minutes, she settled down to licking them as though nothing untoward had happened.

Between calls, I managed to feed the kittens a few times over the day, knowing that Sophie's milk supply would be scant. By the time I was ready to go home that afternoon, Sophie was a different cat, purring loudly and arching her back when petted, which reassured me that she was feeling little, if any, pain.

Remembering my promise to Molly, I packed the trio back into the car and, with Slug sulking in the back, made my way home. That evening, as I fed Fiona, Molly fed her charges, becoming remarkably adept at nudging the tiny feeding bottle into the opened mouths. Gently, she crooned a tuneless lullaby as she sat, legs sticking straight out off the couch, each kitten wrapped in a tiny doll's blanket. Sophie, obviously well used to children, seemed to be quite happy with the arrangement, and jumped up and down every few minutes to check on the progress.

'Her likes me,' declared Molly, pointing her chubby finger in the direction of Sophie.

By the next morning, mother and kittens were making a remarkable recovery. Despite being so underweight, Sophie, freed of her damaged organ, exuded the vitality of a street cat.

By the weekend, her milk was beginning to return significantly and Molly was slightly put out as the kitten chose to return to its mother. It was only then, having spoken to Sandra over the phone, that the problem of returning the little family to their rightful owners arose. Sandra, living some forty miles away, had no form of transport and there was no public service of any sort that came near us. Molly was clearly pleased when we decided that the simplest thing would be for them to stay with us for the week, to be returned the following Wednesday at the next clinic.

Knowing well that the usual handful of Maltesers that I used to bribe Molly to let me go to Ballyfermot wouldn't work this time, I made a quick detour by the toyshop on my way home from work on Tuesday. As though waiting for me, on the first shelf I saw a pink, glittering package, containing a mother cat and a kitten, complete with a tiny feeding bottle.

On the Wednesday evening, with the feline family packed to go, I handed Molly the parcel.

'That's a present from Sophie,' I told her, 'to thank you

for minding her so well.'

Sophie was soon returned to her rightful owners and I didn't hear anything until the following week when she returned to have her stitches out. Her coat was noticeably sleeker and the two kittens were almost unrecognisable as they had developed from scrawny 'rats' to rounded bundles of chocolate-box fluff.

Along with the cats, Sandra had brought a photograph of the happy family for Molly, which Molly insisted on putting in the photograph album alongside Fiona's christening photographs!

CHAPTER NINETEEN

NOT BAD FOR A FIVER!

L ife as a veterinary surgeon, or at least the way in which I practise it, seems, at times, to create a sense of a split personality. Within any single day, I can go from treating some valuable equine, worth (at least in their owner's mind) a significant number of thousand euro, to a stray puppy with no pedigree to his name. Likewise, the owners can span from those with a mouthful of letters after their names to a welfare client that signed the consent form with an undistinguished X. The skill required in the morning might be nothing more than to vaccinate a fluffy kitten, while the afternoon could be spent wrestling with a few tonnes of hefty bovines. It often amuses me, having spent a morning wallowing in blood and muck among a bunch a fractious cattle, to step out of the overalls and into the car and drive away, humming along to some soothing melody on Lyric radio.

In my pre-children days, the journey home might take in the gym for a quick swim and a sauna. The unfortunate fellow-sauna users would also be deceived by the split personality, imagining me as an office worker, grabbing a few moments' peace on the way home, but it would take only a few minutes for the heat of the sauna to release the ingrained scent of bovine that would gradually begin to permeate the confined space. I would close my eyes and lie back so as not to laugh as everyone would start to look around at each other, wondering which of the usual collection of overweight males was the most likely offender!

Wednesday nights added that bit of variety to what was already a varied routine. Donal envied the unpredictability in comparison to his own work where a set job was done on a set day all year through.

'Anything interesting tonight?' he would ask as I arrived back after another busy Wednesday night clinic. The irony was that I often had to think hard to remember even one or two cases that had passed through, such was the frenzied speed of probably one of the busiest Blue Cross clinics in the county.

This particular night, however, I could well remember Derek, one of the regulars who had arrived with his nondescript 'pub terrier'. Monty was well used to the clinic and was usually totally unfazed by the roadside waiting room, crowded with a selection of terriers and mongrels and hissing, spitting felines, all jostling for space. I had often tended not only to his own cuts and bruises from his encounters with the local canines, but more commonly to those he inflicted on others. In general, Monty usually came out best, partly but not solely due to his owner's total refusal to even consider having him neutered. The first time I suggested it the look of shock, pain and disbelief in Monty's owner's eyes made me add, 'It's not you we want to neuter, just your dog!'

Tonight, however, as soon as I stepped down from the van, I noticed that Monty seemed a bit subdued. He stood, with all four legs well apart, back-arched, head down, concentrating hard as he carefully breathed slow, shallow breaths. I was concerned that he didn't seem to be taking any notice of his comrades even when the black and white pit-bull beside him seemed to be shaping up for a fight. Monty just stood, with his tail down, staring intently at the ground.

Unfortunately, his place in the queue meant that it was almost eight-thirty before he was finally carried him up the steps to the van.

Monty gave a little groan as Derek let him down on the table.

'What's up with Monty?' I asked, with genuine concern, as my hands gently probed his tense, enlarged abdomen.

'Don't know, luv,' replied Derek, looking equally concerned. 'Came home from work and me Missis says 'e was lied up in the corner of de box all day.'

The swollen abdomen was rock solid, so solid that I was initially unable to determine the cause.

'Would you know if he passed any urine at all today?' I asked.

'Well, as I says, I wuz workin' meself bu' now dat ye sez it, 'e wasn't peeing outside – ye know de way 'e always does be pissing on ev'ry lamp post wit' all dem udder dogs around.'

As though to confirm my suspicion, Monty stretched down and began to lick frantically at the inflamed penis that emerged from the swollen sheath.

Although the usual cause of blocked bladders are stones formed in the urine, the swelling in the soft tissue suggested a more traumatic cause.

'Any chance he could have been hit by a car or anything?' I asked before giving my worrying diagnosis.

'No way, Doc,' he confirmed. 'The Missus does be dat terrified of de Mont chasing after another dog dat she won't let 'im out.'

I always felt awkward with the next question but it had to be broached. 'Any chance he could have got a kick?' I asked, although knowing Derek and how much he cared for his dog, I wasn't thinking of him.

The look of horror on his face was genuine. 'Ah sure, Doc, who'd kick 'im? D'ye tink some un kicked 'im?' he asked in fury, all in the same breath. 'By God, I'll kill the little bleedin' bollix dat dit it. Who d'ye tink kicked 'im?' he roared at me, getting more agitated as he spoke.

'No. I didn't say anyone kicked him at all, Derek,' I said, trying to calm him and knowing that the conversation was leading us no nearer to treating the dog. Monty moaned softly again and I decided that relieving his discomfort was more important at the moment than worrying about the underlying cause.

By now, Eamon and Gordon were clearly intrigued, knowing well from their years of experience that something unusual was going on.

'The problem is,' I explained to Derek, 'that this swelling here has caused a blockage, so he can't pee anymore.'

Derek looked stumped for a moment. 'So 'ow does he get it out, den?'

'If he can't pass urine, it all stays in the bladder. You see the way he's so swollen here,' I said, indicating the turgid abdomen. 'The bladder can hold a huge volume of water if it has to. In Monty's case, I would guess that he probably hasn't been able to pass water all day and it's all building up inside him.'

'So what do ye do den, Doc?' he asked slowly, not looking too convinced.

'Well, that's the problem, Derek. It's really an emergency that needs to be treated in a clinic. We only have the basics on board here,' I told him, indicating our useful, but limited stock in the ambulance presses.

'What 'as te be done?' he asked, still looking slightly incredulous.

'Well, what they need to do is to pass a catheter, a small plastic tube, into the bladder to try to relieve the blockage.'

'Up 'is bleedin' willy, like?' he asked, subconsciously crossing his legs as though in sympathy with his luckless dog.

'Yes, that right,' I confirmed, stony-faced, fully aware of the renewed interest of the waiting crowd.

'Ah no, Doc, dey couldn't do dat to 'im. Nah, I couldn't let dem,' he added, shaking his head emphatically.

'I'm afraid there's no option, Derek,' I explained. 'You can see he's in terrible pain. You can't leave him like that.'

Derek thought for a moment and then, shaking his head again, replied, 'Ah Jayney, no! No! He'd never be righ' after dat.'

The conversation might have gone on all night if Monty hadn't let out a particularly heart-rending moan, convincing everyone that something needed to be done – and quickly.

In one way I was glad to have the excuse to refer the dog on, as, judging by the tension of his bladder, he was in a bad way. It felt like a good-sized tennis ball in a small terrier's body, bigger than any bladder I had ever felt. The stocks at the clinic didn't stretch to urinary catheters. An emergency clinic would have all the necessary medications and equipment to do a good job on Monty. As always, though, in real life it was never that simple.

Derek's face dropped as I gave him directions to the nearest emergency hospital and gave him a rough idea of the money he would need to bring with him. It was clearly a non-runner.

Time ticked by for poor old Monty as Derek went outside to ring a few of his mates to see if he could make up the money, but minutes later he was no better off. The best he could do was to try to get money from his boss at the weekend. Another feel of Monty's abdomen was enough for me to be sure that the little dog couldn't wait that long.

Rummaging through my bag, I pulled out a fine twenty-one gauge, one and a half-inch needle. I mixed up a solution of hibiscrub and carefully cleaned the hairless portion of the abdomen.

'We have to empty the bladder – one way or another,' I

told Derek. 'This isn't the ideal way of doing it but if we don't release the pressure the bladder is going to burst.'

Derek started to go a bit green underneath his evening stubble when he realised that I was going to drain it through the side of Monty's abdomen. Gordon was ready to take over and deftly restrained the little dog. Eamon stood by with a swab and a hush fell among the expectant onlookers. Having pulled on sterile gloves, I withdrew the needle from its pack and stabbed it through the body wall. Monty never flinched with such a minute pain compared to the intense discomfort that he had been experiencing over the past few hours. Instantly, a gush of deeply coloured urine shot out in a spray, ending on the far window. The onlookers jumped back in amazement as they watched the continuous flow from my needle. Monty appeared to be totally oblivious to the whole procedure and stood panting uncomfortably from the still considerable pressure. Eamon was quick to grab hold of a small dish and by angling my needle, I was able to direct the flow. The hissing of urine on stainless steel continued as everyone stood in amazement, watching the level of red-tinged fluid slowly creep up the container. The steady stream of urine seemed to go on and on. The crowd stood silently, in awe, watching the little dog, who was clearly starting to feel some relief from the slowly subsiding pressure. What had been regular panting broke down to intermittent bouts – the only sound that changed was the continuously deepening pitch of the urine hitting a slowly filling container. When it was almost three-quarters full, Monty, looking around for the first time as though surprised to see a crowd, cautiously at first, wagged his stump of a tail.

Derek's eyes grew wide in awe at the capacity of his beloved pet and eventually blurted out, 'Jayney, de fecker musta been on de Guinness last nigh'!'

The crowd erupted, relieved by the break in tension, and even Monty seemed to join in the general feeling of light-heartedness, his tail now wagging frantically, undoubtedly induced more by the declining size of his rapidly shrinking bladder than from the aspirations regarding his drinking capacity.

As the flow of urine gradually lessened and reduced to a slow drip, I gently forced the bladder upwards to drain as much urine as possible before carefully withdrawing my needle.

'Well, that's the best we can do for him tonight,' I told Derek. I then injected Monty with a suitable antibiotic, which would hopefully sort out any bacteria I might have introduced into the bladder and a strong anti-inflammatory, which I hoped would reduced the swelling in his penis enough to allow him to urinate normally. I poured some of the urine into a sample bottle for further testing at a clinic in the morning, advising Derek to label it carefully in his fridge overnight.

'Keep a close eye on him tonight and ring your local vet first thing in the morning,' I continued.

I sent him off with the appropriate referral letter, wondering what the vet on duty might think of my 'fire--brigade' tactics.

When I saw Derek throw a fiver into the voluntary

donation box on his way out, I wondered whether my basic, but nonetheless effective, intervention might not have been worth a little more.

The last I saw of Monty that night was as he hopped down the steps out of the clinic and immediately launched an attack on a waiting Yorkshire terrier. At least, for the moment, Monty was back to himself, although I knew my treatment was unlikely to be a longterm solution.

Although I remembered to tell Donal about the Monty episode that night, I had all but forgotten it the next Sunday morning when I was in the unusual position of doing a shift for the Dublin emergency clinic. A vet I went to college with worked for them on a regular basis, but due to a family event was unable to do so on that particular day. She rang to see if I would cover for her and I agreed to do it, knowing I was off that weekend myself.

For the first hour or two, I quite enjoyed myself in the purpose-built premises, so different from our own consulting room which served not only the small animal population, but also doubled up as a large-animal treatment room for lambing ewes, replacing prolapses or the odd calf with a fractured limb. I was quite enchanted by the idea of having two fully qualified nurses as my assistants instead of hollering out to Melissa on reception to give a hand whenever things got too chaotic. Eventually, I gave up trying to do anything as the nurses protested whenever I answered the phone or picked up a mop to wash the floors or do any of the hundred and one other mundane things that usually need doing in a veterinary practice. I was sitting back finishing a rare second cup of coffee when the first client came in. I quickly identified the tooth abscess in the cat's upper molar which was causing it such pain. I was delightfully amused to observe that before I had finished filling up the computer record (which admittedly took more time than looking at the cat) that one of the nurses had administered the pain relief and antibiotic injection that I had prescribed and the cat was comfortably set up in a unit and on a drip. Over the next few hours, the clients that trickled in every half hour or so were equally efficiently dealt with by our team. As the clients dwindled off well before lunchtime, I was beginning to appreciate the comfort of the job and wondering if I should go for an unprecedented early lunch.

The computer screen flashed to advise me that I had a new client waiting. In the presenting problem box were the words: 'difficulty in urinating since last Wednesday'. The clinical history reminded me of Monty and I laughed to think of my difference in fortune today. I couldn't believe it when the door opened to admit the same Monty, followed by Derek. His eyes narrowed as he looked as me and then around my auspicious surroundings.

'It is you, isn't it?' he enquired cautiously, as though I were an illusion.

'It's me, all right,' I agreed cheerfully. 'Back in the day job,' I continued, knowing he wouldn't have any idea where I worked normally.

It seemed that Monty had done well on the day after my intervention at the clinic – so well that Derek had ignored my advice to take him to a local clinic for further treatment. However, since Saturday morning, Monty had only been dribbling urine and was almost as blocked as the first night.

Before beginning my shift in the emergency clinic, I had been given instruction in relation to the standard protocol for various conditions. I laboriously typed the clinical history into the computer and in the treatments box ticked the sections for sedation, catheterisation and urinalysis, and put question marks over the blood testing and ultra sound examination – all considered 'best practice' for what can potentially be a very dangerous condition. Derek readily signed the consent form as I explained the reason for the various treatments. Before he left, he handed over the urine sample which appeared not to have left his pocket since the previous Wednesday night. I cringed as I pressed the discharge button which would send the computer generated bill through to reception and ushered Derek out the door while Monty was whisked off by one of the nurses. I couldn't help thinking about the fiver casually thrown in the box on the previous Wednesday. I could just about make out the efficient muted tones of the nurse in reception as she printed out the bill and read out the bottom line.

There was a brief silence before a bellow erupted from Derek: '*How much* to see Dr Hick? But sure, I saw her on Wednesday night and it only cost me a fiver!!'

ALSO BY GILLIAN HICK

VET ON THE LOOSE

Gillian Hick

ALSO BY GILLIAN HICK

Read Gillian's account of her years
as a veterinary student and her earliest
experiences on the job.

About Vet on the Loose:
'Ireland looks set to get its very own
James Herriot ... full of anecdotes and
funny incidents'
Irish Farmer's Journal

'It's an exciting account of the situations
she encounters where the humans are
often more problematic than the animals,
particularly the guys who want to know:
Where is the real vet?'
Irish Independent

'Very well written in an easy-flowing
style' *Irish Farmer's Journal*

'Gillian is a young vet with a lively sense
of humour and a pleasant, easy-going writing style ... animal lovers will be well
pleased with her pacy anecdotes'
Irish Examiner

OTHER BOOKS FROM O'BRIEN PRESS

Michael Kelly once worked in the city, then he and his wife decided to change their lifestyle. When they moved to a somewhat leaky country cottage in Dunmore East, they began to grow a few vegetables – and even started to keep hens and pigs! This book tells of the first shaky steps away from the old life into the new, described with humour and affection.

ISBN 978-1-84717-070-5

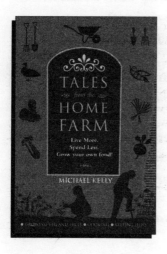

Five years on – an invaluable and timely guide to self-sufficiency at home: growing your own food, cooking, storing, keeping animals, and lots more, dispensed with humour and tales of the author's own successes and failures. Perfect for the novice grower, with tips and plans to take you through the year. Full of suggestions and encouragement.

ISBN 978-1-84717-168-9

OTHER BOOKS FROM O'BRIEN PRESS

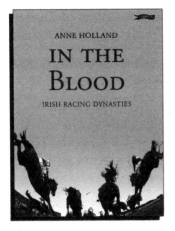

There are Irish families for whom horseracing truly is in the blood. Families of jockeys and trainers like the Walshes and Geraghtys, families who photograph racing, commentate and take bets, like the O'Hehirs, Healys and Grahams. And, of course, there are the star horses.
Lavishly illustrated with over a hundred photographs.

ISBN 978-1-84717-180-1

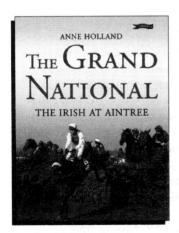

The Aintree Grand National is the world's most famous horserace and from its earliest years Irish horses, jockeys, trainers and breeders have been prominent there.
A wonderfully illustrated and compulsively readable account of a beloved institution.

ISBN 978-1-84717-074-3

OTHER BOOKS FROM O'BRIEN PRESS

A marvellous collection of over seventy biographies, detailing the lives of extraordinary women from Ireland's past – from pirates to patriots, warriors to writers, mistresses to male impersonators.

ISBN 978-0-86278-780-6

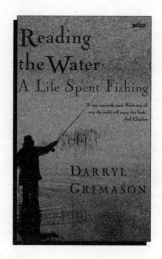

TV presenter Darryl Grimason conveys the passion for fishing that has inspired him since boyhood. From angling for wild brown trout on Lough Corrib to the capture of a giant bluefin tuna off the Donegal coast, his enthusiasm for the subject is infectious.

ISBN 978-0-86278-914-5